GANGSTER WOMEN

GANGSTER WOMEN

AND THE CRIMINALS THEY LOVED

Susan McNicoll

ARCTURUS

Corbis Images: 11 (top) (Bettmann); 11 (bottom) (Underwood
& Underwood); 52 (Bettmann); 76 (Bettmann); 83 (Bettmann); 89
(Bettmann); 155 (Bettmann); 164 (Bettmann); 167 (Bettmann);
Federal Bureau of Investigation: 93; 103;
Getty Images: 66 (New York Daily News Archive); 120 (Hulton Archive);
175 (New York Daily News Archive)
Shutterstock: 22 (Everett Historical); 35 (Everett Historical); 41
(Everett Historical); 46 (Everett Historical); 59 (Everett Historical); 147
(Everett Historical);
Topfoto: 149 (AP)

ARCTURUS

This edition published in 2016 by Arcturus Publishing Limited
26/27 Bickels Yard, 151–153 Bermondsey Street,
London SE1 3HA

ISBN: 978-1-78599-125-7
DA004723US

Printed in China

CONTENTS

For Jay, my cat and my muse for everything important in life. You have a crazy sense of humor and piercing green eyes that see more truth than those of most humans. Thank you for choosing me.

Introduction

When I first became interested in the women who chose to ride alongside the gangsters of the early 1930s, I was hoping to find one underlying psychological reason for their choices. It turned out to be more complicated than that. I also found a distinct difference between the women known as gangster molls and their later mobster counterparts.

I wrote about only one mobster moll because I found the gangsters' women more interesting. The exception was Virginia Hill, who straddled the line between mistress and criminal herself and ended up dead in mysterious circumstances. That I found intriguing. But these mobster molls were a different breed of women entirely than their gangster equivalents. They were mostly in it for the money and the fame of being with a mobster. Love rarely mattered.

Not so for the gangster molls, who often greatly loved their men, having children with them, and sometimes marrying them. In many ways these women were influenced by both the flapper era and the Great Depression which devastated the United States following the Wall Street Crash of October 29, 1929 (also known as Black Tuesday) and ravaged the country for many years.

The flapper era of the 1920s, with its disregard for convention, brought about a change in fashion and sexuality and a redefinition of women's roles in society. The media saw the flapper women as pleasure-loving, reckless and also convention-defying by initiating sexual relationships. They were a force to be reckoned with, as they now voted and went out to work.

The Depression ended this extravagant era, but much of the change in fashion, attitude and society's view of women lingered. The times were now desperate, which meant that most people were eager for something glamorous and exciting to focus on, and the press gave it to them in the form of the women they called gun molls. The exploits of the gangsters were chronicled and when many of the women were later arrested for harboring their men the press described them in detail, from the clothes they were wearing to the style of their hair. The public couldn't get enough.

The term "gun moll" became popular in the early 1930s and implied that the women actually fired the guns, when in fact they almost never used the firearms themselves. Bonnie Parker and Helen Gillis (wife of Lester "Baby Face" Nelson) were among the few women who even handled the guns—but only to load them for their men.

The real Bonnie and Clyde, and the "reel" version where the gangsters were portrayed by Faye Dunaway and Warren Beatty. The photos show how the movie faithfully reconstructed what was to become their mythic pose.

Bonnie and Clyde highlighted the beginning of this brief period of the gangsters and their molls, and Bonnie did much to shape the way these women were viewed. The photos taken of her in a dress holding a cigar or a gun became legendary. She looked glamorous and totally in charge.

But the gangster moll painted in the press was a far cry from reality. Bonnie owned only a couple of outfits. Gangsters never looked long enough into the future to plan wardrobes. They stole enough money to get them by for a short while and then robbed again. Sometimes they wanted to settle down, but most knew their crimes were going to lead to jail or death—and their women knew it too.

Asked by the judge why she left her children to go on the run with her husband, Lester "Baby Face" Nelson, Helen Gillis replied, "Well, I knew Les didn't have very long to live and I wanted to be with him just as long as I could."

When the money was there, the molls did buy clothes and jewelry, but most of it was left behind soon after when the law got too close and they had to escape. In running, the men often left the women behind as well, to be picked up later if possible.

Like Bonnie, the women sometimes lived with only one outfit for days or weeks at a time and knew how to stretch a dollar and treat wounds. Helen and Lester often slept outside in the mountains while on the run. The women were glorified gofers, used to buy and transport vehicles, shuffle money from one gangster to another, or to pay a bribe. In a way, they were disposable even though their partners often were truly in love with them.

So why did these women do it? The easy answer is that they loved their men as much as they were loved. But I think the era they lived in had a big influence, too. Their lives at home in the Depression were miserable, so when love seemed to come along they jumped at it. Some were drawn from their dreary lives by the excitement. In one case a moll pulled her two younger siblings into the lifestyle. Another moll was the stereotypical abused woman, pregnant and terrified to leave.

This was also a time before the FBI as we know it existed and their powers as the Division of Investigation were limited during most of the period of this book. However, that didn't prevent the man heading the organization, J. Edgar Hoover, from blaming the women for much of what the men did. He even cited them as being more dangerous to society than the gangsters themselves. This was ridiculous, as the women had virtually no power over the crimes the men committed.

Hoover was angered by the leniency shown by the

courts toward these molls. There was a reason for this, though—public opinion. As the U.S. Attorney's Office stated, in citing the acquittal of a gangster's wife, the jury believed "she was a woman, therefore dominated and coerced into the life by her husband." Because of this belief a number of the women were never initially prosecuted.

I first looked at the gangsters, starting with Clyde Barrow and the woman who travelled by his side, Bonnie Parker. This led me to wonder if other women had died with their men and I researched most of the interesting gangsters of the day and the women they took on the ride with them. I thought the women might be inconsequential to these men, but on closer examination I saw that there were very strong bonds, and I chose the most intriguing unions of these.

The scale of the gangster era—the numbers of criminals and molls—was facilitated partly by the desperation that existed across the land due to the Depression, but it was also a time of limited communications, in general and between different law agencies. The gangs of today are just as attractive to vulnerable youths and certainly just as violent, but they are not glamorized in the press the way gangsters were in the early 1930s.

The posed photographs of Bonnie with her cigar

or pointing a gun at Clyde did not show the uglier side of their journey. The Division of Investigation's Wanted poster for Bonnie Parker clearly described her acquisitions during her time with Clyde:

"Scars and marks, bullet wound left foot next to little toe; bullet in left knee; burn scar on right leg from hip to knee."

Life on the run was far from a picnic.

Chapter One

NO VACATIONS WITH GANGSTERS

The guests arriving at Little Bohemia Lodge in northern Wisconsin on Friday, April 20, 1934, weren't asking for much. A few days of peace and quiet. A break from looking over their shoulders. Time to settle into a brief period of domesticity. It was only to be a short vacation, but all of them needed it, especially the women.

Only a few weeks earlier, the group—remnants of the recently busted Dillinger gang—had met at Louie's Roadhouse on the highway in Fox River Grove, Illinois, about 40 miles northwest of Chicago. Louie Cernocky, a jovial restaurateur, was happy to have the gang make his place their headquarters for a few days.

A failed police trap to capture John Dillinger in Chicago earlier that month had resulted in his girlfriend, Evelyn Frechette, being taken into custody. Her arrest had left Dillinger very depressed; his dreams of going into hiding with her somewhere far away were shattered. With Chicago now the center of an intense search for Dillinger, it seemed wise for him and his colleagues to skip town. They needed a hideout and Cernocky, a friend of Lester "Baby Face" Nelson, knew just the place.

Little Bohemia Lodge sat on the edge of Little Star Lake in a small community 13 miles south of Mercer, Wisconsin. The owner, Emil Wanatka, had strong connections with the underworld in Chicago. Ten years earlier, using money he'd made as a bootlegger during the early years of prohibition, Wanatka had purchased a restaurant on Chicago's North Side. It attracted sports celebrities such as boxers Jack Dempsey and Gene Tunney, as well as becoming a favorite with the likes of gangster "Bugsy" Moran and his North Side Gang. Much of this popularity was thanks to Wanatka's connections on both sides of the law, which handily let him get away with openly serving alcohol.

Business boomed for several years before souring. First, the St. Valentine's Day Massacre in 1929 killed off many of the clientele. Six members of Moran's gang plus a doctor were gunned down in a Chicago garage, an event that effectively wiped out the North Side gang and the flow of money into Wanatka's restaurant. And then the Depression hit, forcing Wanatka to sell. His wife, Nan, wanted to move back to her home community in Wisconsin. Finally, Wanatka acquiesced and a year later opened his lodge.

Little Bohemia was built of timbers, in a rustic Alpine style. It was set back 1,200 feet from the only access road, Highway 51, and surrounded by woods. The ground floor was composed of a dining room, large kitchen, parlor with a fireplace, and a bar. The décor ran to wood paneling and mounted hunting trophies—stuffed heads of moose and other local wildlife. Upstairs were eight bedrooms. In addition to the main building, several guest cabins were located on the property.

Although busy with this new enterprise, Wanatka still had time for some of his Chicago cronies (much to his wife's disgust). One of his closest friends was Louie Cernocky, who often sent business Wanatka's way. This was how Dillinger and nine others came to be there that snowy weekend in 1934, deep in Wisconsin lake country.

At 2:30 p.m. on Friday, April 20, a black Ford pulled up to the lodge. Homer Van Meter stepped out of the driver's side. He was shortly followed by his girlfriend, Marie "Mickey" Comforti, holding her Boston bull terrier, and another passenger, Pat Reilly. They trudged across the cold driveway and entered the lobby of the lodge. Introducing himself as Wayne, Van Meter asked Wanatka if they could have a late lunch. He also explained that they were going to be joined shortly by seven others, one of whom would be bringing a letter of introduction from Louie Cernocky. Could Wanatka accommodate that many guests for a few days? Only too happy for the business, Wanatka assured him he could and hurried to prepare the rooms.

Later that afternoon a Ford sedan arrived, carrying John Dillinger (his hair dyed a shade of red that looked more like orange), John Hamilton, and the latter's girlfriend, Pat Cherrington. They were followed half an hour later by a third car, driven by Tommy Carroll. With him were his girlfriend, Jean Delaney Crompton, and Lester "Baby Face" Nelson and his wife, Helen Gillis.

Nelson, a short, sandy-haired young man, introduced himself to Wanatka as Jimmie. When he handed him Cernocky's note, the lodge owner got the picture right away. This was no ordinary group of weekenders. They had to be from the underworld. Although he did not know it at the time, here, under his roof, he would be harboring five of the most wanted men in the United States—and one (Reilly) who liked to pretend he was one of them.

Underworld or not, Wanatka wasn't about to let his friend Cernocky down—nor turn away guests with such deep pockets.

That first evening, Reilly, Carroll, Dillinger, Nelson, and Wanatka played cards in the parlor. None of the gangsters was drinking, as they were keeping themselves clear-headed in case of trouble. The past few weeks had made them all tense, and even way out here so far from Chicago they knew they couldn't be too careful.

While the men played . . .

As the men chatted and carried on with their game, the four women did what was usually expected of them: they hung out in the background. Mickey, a city girl, was fidgety and feeling out of place in the isolated country setting.

Jean, newly pregnant, was very much under the control of her boyfriend, Carroll. He wouldn't let her drink or socialize much with the others, so she spent a lot of her time in their room. Pat, too, had gone off to her room. She was in a lot of discomfort from recent surgery. That left Helen to keep Mickey company in the parlor. Helen, at 5 foot 2 inches and weighing little more than 90 pounds, may have been small but—like her husband, "Baby Face" Nelson—she was tough. A no-makeup, no-jewelry, no-nonsense kind of a woman, she was the alpha female of the group, telling the other women what to do. And like the men, she was also ever-vigilant about betrayal. She trusted no one.

John Dillinger and his infamous stare.

The card game ended around midnight and everyone headed off to bed. Nelson and Helen shared one of the two-bedroom cabins with Carroll and Jean. All the others slept in the main lodge building, with Reilly and Dillinger sharing a room. When Reilly entered their room on the first night, Dillinger was stretched out on his bed reading a detective magazine.

After Wanatka went to bed following the card game that night, Nan drilled him about the guests.

"I think the fellow with the dyed hair is Dillinger," he told her. While Nan was no stranger to the shady parts of her husband's past, this news was more than she was prepared for. She demanded Wanatka do something about it.

After breakfast the next morning, Wanatka spoke with Dillinger privately. Standing in his office, he told the fugitive that he knew who he was and expressed concern that there might be a "shooting match" at his lodge. Dillinger assured Wanatka that wouldn't happen. A rest and hideaway for a few days was the group's only interest. Dillinger also assured Wanatka that he'd be well paid and then he and his group would be on their way.

Whether Wanatka was truly afraid or just humoring his wife is unclear. (In a photograph of him with Dillinger, taken that weekend, Wanatka is smiling broadly, an arm draped around the gangster's shoulder. Dillinger looks glum, his arms folded across his chest.) Nan, however, was definitely afraid, especially for the safety of her young son, Emil Jr. She knew that word had already spread through the small town about a group of guests with expensive cars showing up at Little Bohemia. This attention, Nan feared, could only lead to trouble.

For their part, Dillinger and his men kept a sharp eye on the comings and goings of the lodge's staff. If anyone had to leave the property for any reason, one of the gangsters would discreetly follow at a distance. It was a plan they did not stick to later, much to their loss. When Nan headed to the rooms Saturday morning to change bedding, Nelson stopped her, sure he had caught her snooping. He took his suspicions to Dillinger, who told him not to worry about it. Dillinger trusted Wanatka up to a point, but he did say to one of his lawyers much later about the lodge, "You couldn't whisper your own thoughts to your pillow without Mrs. Wanatka knowing all about it ten minutes afterward."

Pat Cherrington had arrived at the lodge in a great deal of pain from recent surgery for a ventral hernia. This pain in her stomach increased to such an extent that after breakfast she decided that she needed to see a doctor. She went to the others to ask for a ride into town and found out that Reilly was being sent on an errand to St. Paul, Minnesota. Pat asked to join him so that she could see a specialist and they left together shortly after noon, intending to return by nightfall on Sunday.

The two lodge employees, George Bazso and Frank Traube, both had a good idea who they were dealing with, but still found the gangsters easy to get along with. Calling Dillinger "a typical Indiana farm boy," Bazso later said he was surprised that Dillinger got so much media attention because it seemed as if the others were in charge. While the men were personable, Bazso said, he kept his distance from the women "because of who their men were."

Traube, on the Saturday afternoon, even offered to show Nelson and Carroll around the property. When someone suggested target practice (and the guests just happened to have firearms on hand), Traube set a can upright in the snow. Carroll merely nicked it with his .38, while Nelson, using his .45, pumped every bullet into the can. Shortly after that, Wanatka, Dillinger and Van Meter all joined them and the group moved 80 yards away to take shots with a rifle. Only Wanatka and Van Meter were able to hit it at that distance.

Back at the lodge, Nan was plotting

Nan was becoming increasingly determined to get her son away, and the perfect excuse for making that happen soon presented itself. Her brother, George LaPorte, was having a birthday party for his son at their home two miles from Little Bohemia. Nan told her husband and Dillinger that it would look suspicious if the boy didn't leave to attend the party. Dillinger was happy to have the boy go and even handed him a quarter. Wanatka, who was taking Van Meter to town to drop off the gang's laundry, drove Emil Jr. to the party at the same time.

After he got back, Wanatka and Nan had a serious discussion about the situation. He was torn: he knew he should alert the authorities, yet he was afraid that if he did it would lead to a shootout— not to mention some awkward questions about him knowingly harboring criminals at the lodge. To cover his back, Wanatka finally decided that the thing to do was to send a letter to a friend in Chicago who was an assistant district attorney. By the time the letter got there, Dillinger and his friends would be long gone. Alternatively, if the gangsters were discovered at Little Bohemia, Wanatka could point to the letter to show he'd tried to tell someone. He quickly wrote the letter and Nan hid it in her clothes and looked for a way off the property. One of her guests provided the opportunity.

As Nan began to prepare dinner that Saturday evening, Helen Gillis offered to help. When Nan casually mentioned how much she wished she had gone with her son to the birthday party, Helen urged her to go then, saying that she and the other women could take care of the dinner. Nan approached the male guests, who were beginning the evening's card games with her husband, and none of them had any objection to her heading off for a while. She wasted no time in leaving.

Snowflakes were falling as Nan drove along Highway 51. She picked up another brother, Lloyd, and on the way to the party, she blurted out the whole story. Their first order of business was to mail her husband's letter. The second was to involve their brother-in-law, Henry Voss.

It was evening when Nan and the three men huddled in a bedroom at her brother's George's house and came up with a plan. Because there were no private phone lines nearby, Voss volunteered to drive to Rhinelander, 50 miles south of Little Bohemia, to notify federal authorities. He wanted to leave right away, but Nan insisted that she should talk things over with her husband first. It was agreed that Lloyd would find some inconspicuous reason to drop by the lodge first thing in the morning to get a sign to proceed. With that, Nan headed back home, leaving her son safely with his relatives.

At 7:15 a.m. the next morning, Sunday, April 22, there was Lloyd on the doorstep of Little Bohemia, his mother in tow. By the time they left half an hour later, Nan had slipped her brother a package of cigarettes. In the package was a note telling Voss to go ahead.

By 10:00 a.m., Voss and Lloyd had pulled into Rhinelander and found a phone. It took Voss almost two hours to get through to anyone in authority willing to take control of the situation. Finally he succeeded in reaching the US Marshal in Chicago and was told the Justice Department was handling the Dillinger case. He gave the Marshal the number he was at and asked that someone in the Justice Department contact him, and soon. In no time Voss got his call returned by Melvin Purvis.

"Nervous Purvis," as his contemporaries called him, oversaw the Chicago office of the Division of Investigation—the organization that would become the FBI less than two years later.

"He was a small man with bright, alert eyes who dressed fashionably and was so fastidious he often changed shirts three times a day [and] spoke with a polite, pleasant drawl," author John Toland wrote of

Purvis in *The Dillinger Days*. "One might have thought he was a successful young bond salesman perhaps . . . but certainly not a G-Man [government agent]. He was a competent executive, a man of unquestioned courage despite his excitability, and was well liked by those who worked under him."

Purvis was the protégé of J. Edgar Hoover, head of the Division of Investigation, and could do no wrong (at least, up until the point when Purvis began to get the attention Hoover wanted for himself—a fact that later led to Purvis's downfall). It was Hoover who had put Purvis in a position of authority and power, promoting him in December 1932 to head up the Chicago office. And so it was Purvis to whom Voss's call was directed.

"The man you want most is up here," Voss said to Purvis over the phone that Sunday afternoon in 1934. Neither one of them had to say John Dillinger was that man.

On hearing the details about the gathering at Little Bohemia, Purvis quickly moved into action. He'd been criticized by Hoover recently for his failure to nab Dillinger and here was a chance to redeem himself. When he learned from Voss that the nearest airport to his quarry was in Rhinelander, Purvis chartered two planes to be ready for take-off within an hour. He then spoke to Hoover, who told him to phone the St. Paul office and order up extra manpower. All the agents were to meet in Rhinelander and take it from there. The St. Paul contingent was led by Hugh Clegg, Assistant Director of the Division of Investigation, and Special Agent William Rorer. Three other agents joined them. They reached Rhinelander first. Voss met Clegg at the airport and drew a diagram for him of the layout of the lodge. Just before dusk, the two planes carrying Purvis, eleven additional agents, and weapons arrived. Meanwhile, a host of other agents from St. Paul and Chicago had been dispatched to the scene by car. The government forces were taking up their positions for battle.

Purvis prepares to take down Dillinger

Five cars were rustled up to take the seventeen agents from Rhinelander to Mercer. Because it was now about 6:00 p.m., the plan was to swoop in during the early hours of Monday morning. Voss told the agents that the Wanatkas had prearranged with him that they and their employees would hide in the lodge's basement at 4:00 a.m. so the agents could conduct the raid without concern of harming them. Things were falling into place nicely for Purvis.

Back at Little Bohemia, however, events had taken an unexpected turn. Sunday evenings, the lodge served a special dinner-for-a-dollar and dozens of patrons regularly showed up for the meal between 4:00 and 7:00 p.m. Dillinger—perhaps for this reason or perhaps because the weather had turned very cold and windy—had already decided he was not going to stay over Sunday night. He settled the group's bill with Wanatka (paying him almost double what was owed) and asked for an early dinner for all of them. Dillinger was expecting Reilly and Pat Cherrington back any minute. After dinner, the plan was that some of them would then leave. Only Nelson, Helen, Carroll, and Jean would stay one more night and leave as originally planned on Monday morning.

This sudden change of schedule by his guests threw Wanatka into a panic. Up to that point, he and the government agents were sure they had until Monday to carry out the ambush. How was he now going to alert the agents without giving anything away? He had no way of contacting them. As luck would have it, however, yet one more member of Nan's family—this time, her sister Ruth Voss—showed up at the lodge to check on things. When she heard about Dillinger's impending departure, she headed straight to Rhinelander to sound the alarm. She met her husband on the road as he was driving home after leaving the agents. He immediately turned around again and raced back to tell Purvis what was happening. The attack plan was moved up, with the assault now to take place as soon as the agents could reach the lodge and surround it. The vehicles and weapons coming from Chicago and St. Paul had not yet arrived, so the men loaded what weapons and ammunition they had into the five cars and sped down the highway toward Little Star Lake.

After returning home, Ruth Voss reached Nan by phone and, as carefully as possible in case they were being overheard, persuaded her to leave and come to the safety of their home. Nan hastily told her husband she had to go and see her sister and left, hoping none of the gangsters had overheard her. They hadn't.

Twenty miles away from the lodge, one of the agents' vehicles broke down. Its occupants and weapons had to be jammed into the other four cars. Five miles later, a tire blew on another vehicle. Time being of the essence now, Clegg ordered eight of the agents to climb onto the running boards of the remaining three vehicles. Weighted down by their 24-pound bullet-proof vests, the agents traveled the last 15 miles along the bumpy road clinging to the sides of the cars in bitterly cold weather.

Still, they knew what to do on arrival. Some agents would storm through the front door flanked on both the left and right sides of the lodge by other groups. Unfortunately, Henry Voss had unwittingly left out several vital details in drawing his diagram for the agents: the steep embankment between the rear of the lodge and the lake; the deep ditch on the left of the lodge; the barbed wire fence on the right; and the two resident dogs.

At 8:45 p.m., the agents jumped out of their cars and began to move toward the lodge. Nelson had gone to his cabin, but his wife, Helen, and Jean were not yet ready for bed. Helen persuaded Jean to leave the cabin with her, so they put sweaters over their pajamas and returned to the main lodge, calling upstairs for Mickey to join them in a card game. Dillinger, Hamilton, and Van Meter, still waiting for Reilly's return, were at the bar with Carroll. Suddenly, the dogs began to bark. Dillinger's group, now used to their barking after a couple of days at the lodge, paid little attention to the ruckus. The agents, on the other hand, panicked and thought their cover had been blown. They ran, stumbling, to get into position.

At that moment, the last three dinner-for-a-dollar guests came out of the lodge to head home: Eugene Boiseneau, John Morris, and John Hoffman. They were followed out the front door by Traube and Bazso, who wanted to see why the dogs were continuing to bark. The agents, chilled through in the frigid air and now unnerved by the dogs, were convinced the three men walking to their car were members of the gang.

"Stick 'em up!" cried out one of the agents precisely as the three diners climbed into Hoffman's car and the radio came on at full volume. (Both Traube and Wanatka, who by now was on the porch too, heard someone shout "Stick 'em up" even though official government reports recorded what was said as "Stop, Federal Agents!") Hoffman began to drive off, possibly thinking he was dealing with would-be robbers.

Machine guns and at least one shotgun opened fire. Close to 30 bullets ripped through the car. "It was just like a big windstorm," Hoffman later recalled. He hit the brakes and the windows shattered around him, cutting his face as he tried to duck. One bullet grazed his arm and another cut into his leg. Somehow he managed to escape from the car and stagger into the woods. Morris suffered two shots through his shoulder and another to a kidney but, fueled by alcohol, he stumbled out of the car and then sat down, leaning up against it. He pulled a flask from his back pocket and took a swig. Gunsmoke and powder still filled the air as a swing tune from the radio filled the momentary silence.

Then, as Purvis reported it, "a bullet hit the ground a yard from my right foot, and two other bullets struck trees behind me." They'd been fired by Nelson from the cabin, and reportedly were the only ones fired by any of the gangsters at the agents that night at Little Bohemia.

The gangsters make their escape

Inside the lodge, Dillinger had been up and moving at the first crack of gunfire, followed instantly by Van Meter, Carroll, and Hamilton. They all leaped from the second floor into the snow and found a handy escape route down the unprotected steep embankment at the rear of the lodge. After shooting at Purvis, Nelson made a hasty escape too—one that involved killing a police officer a few miles away.

Little Bohemia as it looked a couple of days after the escape of John Dillinger and his cohorts in April 1934.

The only member of Dillinger's party to be injured during the raid was one of the women. Just when the government agents were getting into place and the action was about to begin, Reilly and Pat Cherrington showed up. They drove down the lane toward the lodge and stopped their car behind the agents, some of whom raced toward it, ordering them out. Reilly rammed the car into reverse and backed up at full speed down the driveway as the agents opened fire at them. A bullet shattered the window, grazing Pat's eye and fracturing her arm. But in spite of a flat tire which had been punctured by bullets, Pat and Reilly escaped.

When the shooting first started, Bazso and Traube ran back into the lodge and, with Wanatka, raced to hide in the cellar. They were beaten there by Helen, Jean, and Mickey, who had been abandoned by their men as soon as the trouble started. The six of them hid in the coal bin—the women, Bazso would later say, calmer than the men, no doubt thanks to their experience of living with gangsters. Outside, Morris staggered to his feet and made his way into the lodge, where he phoned the local telephone operator to report that the place had been "held up." Both he and Hoffman survived the shooting, but Boiseneau, the third innocent occupant of the car, was not so lucky. He was killed instantly by the agents' gunfire.

Purvis and Clegg still believed they had at least some of the gang trapped in the lodge. They sent two agents off to inform J. Edgar Hoover of this, and he promptly announced to the press that agents had Dillinger and his gang "trapped in a remote Wisconsin roadhouse." There was no mention of killing an innocent bystander and wounding two others.

At about 9:30 p.m., Wanatka and his two employees left the women in the cellar and crept upstairs. Supporting a bleeding Morris, they all ventured outside with their arms raised. The agents refused to believe them when they said that only three of the gang's women remained inside.

By this time, the back-up agents from St. Paul and Chicago had finally arrived by car, bringing with them tear gas canisters. It was almost dawn as Purvis ordered the final assault. The canisters were thrown into the lodge while the agents readied themselves outside to receive the flushed-out gangsters.

Minutes later they heard a woman's voice calling, "We'll come out if you promise not to shoot!"

Their eyes watering and swollen from the tear gas, the women, two of them pajama-clad and the third, Mickey, clutching her terrier in her arms, appeared in the doorway. Agents attired in gas masks stormed the building. It was indeed empty.

The battle of Little Bohemia was over. For all their efforts, the government forces had managed to nab only three small women, deserted unceremoniously by the men they loved.

Chapter Two

HELEN GILLIS AND LESTER "BABY FACE" NELSON

Who were these women who risked everything to stay with the men of the underworld?

In the aftermath of their arrest at Little Bohemia Lodge, Mickey Comforti told a reporter, "Don't call us molls when you write your story. We hate that!" Her request fell on deaf ears, for when they were not being called "girls" or "paramours" in the press, they were definitely being called molls. The word originated in the 1600s, when it was a diminutive of "Mary"—a euphemism for prostitute. Fast forward to the 1930s and "molls" had become a press favorite to refer to the women who hung out with gangsters.

"Molls Under $150,000 Bail," blared the headline in Wisconsin's *Capital Times* on April 25, 1934. The interrogations and arraignments of Mickey, Helen Gillis, and Jean Delaney Crompton were shrouded in secrecy and no photographers were allowed near them. However, the photos taken when the three were first taken into custody were all over the papers. The women were shown shielding their faces from the cameras with handkerchiefs—out of modesty, according to reporters, when in fact they were simply dabbing their eyes after the tear gas assault at Little Bohemia.

Helen, Jean, and Mickey were arrested under a newly enacted law that made harboring a federal fugitive a criminal offense. In their case, the three were charged with harboring John Dillinger. The women were kept apart and deprived of food and sleep by federal agents who were desperate to get them to reveal the whereabouts of their gangster boyfriends. The agents also wanted to find out who the women really were. When arrested, all three had given fictitious names to throw officials off the scent. They finally did give up their names, but not those of their lovers. Four days later, the women were still dressed as they had been on the night of the raid. Much was made of the silk pajamas worn by Helen and Jean, and many erroneous stories about all of the women made their way into print—some of them generated by the molls themselves.

"This is a sequel to a honeymoon as adventurous as any girl ever had . . . spent with one of the five gangsters who, leaving a trail of 13 ruthless murders through the Middle West, blasted their way out of a trap," an article in the *Capital Times* said about Helen.

Marie Comforti, Helen Gillis, and the newly pregnant Jean Delaney Crompton shortly after their arrest at Little Bohemia.

"The only part of her trousseau she has is her lounging pajamas, now a little soiled from the wear and tear of four days spent in two jails . . . her 'Honeymoon Hotels'." In truth, Helen had by that time been married to Lester "Baby Face" Nelson for five years and they had two children.

While the public was intrigued by these women, J. Edgar Hoover, head of the Federal Division of Investigation, was decidedly not. Apart from believing (with no evidence to back it up) that any woman connected to the underworld carried syphilis and gonorrhea, Hoover proclaimed in reference to the moll: "She is more dangerous to society than the desperado himself." He was certainly convinced that these three were responsible for the gangsters' escape at the lodge (neglecting to say how much his own agents' incompetence also had to do with it).

Hoover's ranting against the gun molls did have some grounds. To his extreme frustration, women connected with gangsters were usually dealt very light sentences considering the crimes to which they were accessories. Memos from him at the time when Helen, Jean, and Mickey were taken into custody ordered his agents to withhold food and sleep until they talked.

Deep in hiding, Nelson was frantic to get Helen out of jail and asked his sister to go to the prison in Madison to see her. She was startled to find Helen ill, with dark circles under her eyes and a pallor to her skin. Helen admitted she had not eaten or slept well since her arrival, and she was in tears talking about her children and husband.

"They'll get him, you know," she told her sister-in-law. "It won't be long either. I just want to spend all my time with him before the end comes."

Soon after that, Helen was confined to bed by doctors who found her malnourished and gravely anemic. However, she recovered in time to appear before a judge in late May. All three women pleaded guilty and the judge sentenced them to eighteen months' probation.

"The court is satisfied that while these girls are technically guilty, they didn't do anything to aid in the concealment of Dillinger," announced the judge in closing the case. Hoover, who had expected them to receive jail time, was furious and ordered surveillance of all three of them.

Helen, although still exhausted and run down, was just happy to be out and going home to see her children. She was, however, still very despondent on the train heading out of Madison. Bonnie and Clyde, two other famous gangsters of the time, had just been gunned down by federal agents in Texas. As Helen read the newspaper account of their burials, she remarked to Jean that she thought it was "romantic" the couple had died together.

While Bonnie and Clyde were seen by the public as the Romeo and Juliet of the Depression era gangsters, Helen and "Baby Face" Nelson could have been considered close seconds. The occasional abandonment of his family by Nelson notwithstanding (part of the nature of his business), they were devoted to each other. It had been that way from the beginning.

Helen and "Baby Face" Nelson meet

In the spring of 1928, Helen Wawrzyniak, who had just turned fifteen, was in high school and working part time in Goldblatt's department store in Chicago. She had been a sickly child and her life in recent years had been difficult. Her parents, Kasmira and Vincent Wawrzyniak, were of Polish descent and immigrated to the United States from Germany. Both her mother and her older sister were dead, so many of the family's domestic responsibilities had fallen on Helen's shoulders. The young man who came into her life then was a breath of fresh air.

Eighteen years old, Lester Gillis (as Nelson was born) stood 5 feet 5 inches tall and had soft blue eyes, light brown wavy hair, and a cherubic look that he never outgrew. The latter had earned him the nickname he would hate to the end—Baby Face.

Born December 6, 1908 and doted on as the youngest of seven children, Lester was a free spirit who early on became involved with gang members in The Patch, a notorious area of Chicago. Small but wiry, Lester soon had a reputation for using his fists. His parents, immigrants from Belgium, were at a loss to control him. He loved to drive and his "borrowing" of neighborhood cars led to a stint in the St. Charles Reformatory for boys. On his release, it seemed as though Lester turned his life around, but that didn't last. Although his father had been a successful tanner, family circumstances changed, leading Gillis Sr. to depression and drink. As the family struggled, Lester couldn't resist being pulled back into his old habits, and that led to a return to St. Charles.

While he was there, his father committed suicide, on Christmas Eve 1924. Lester was allowed to attend the funeral before returning to the reformatory, but he was wracked with guilt over his father's death. That feeling, and a decision to abstain from alcohol, stayed with him for the rest of his life.

Lester was an exemplary inmate, seen as likeable and bright, and after his second release, he got a legitimate job as a mechanic and stuck with it for more than a year. Still, he was unable to resist the lure of the underworld life—just as he was unable to resist the woman he spent the rest of his days with.

"The moment he met Helen," Lester's mother once said, "there was never room for any other girl

The youthful looking Lester "Baby Face" Nelson, already well on his way down the road of a life of crime.

in his thoughts." And there never would be. The man who became "Baby Face" Nelson and one of America's most wanted criminals was exceptionally unusual in that regard.

By the end of the summer of 1928, Helen was pregnant. The young couple saved their money and eloped, marrying on October 30. The marriage certificate said he was twenty-one and she was twenty. Their son was born in April 1929, followed by a daughter in the summer of 1930. Lester became determined to buy his family a house. He was by most accounts a strong family man who loved to be at home with his wife and children.

How he reconciled this with his unsavory business life is hard to say. Helen knew from the beginning what he was up to, but she loved him so much that she was willing to move constantly, leave her children behind when necessary, and live with the knowledge that death could come to them in an instant. She became as skilled as her husband in eluding police. Years later she said she would have done anything to stay with Les—and she did.

In late 1929 and early 1930, three separate robberies in the wealthy suburbs of Chicago made headlines. The intruders entered the homes, tied up the occupants, and stole cash and jewelry worth thousands of dollars. Lester was a part of these heists and when, in April 1930, he moved his family into a new apartment, he began to introduce himself to neighbors as George Nelson. From this point forward, Lester Gillis ceased to exist, although Helen still called him "Les" and always referred to herself in the future as Helen Gillis.

Bank robbery was Nelson's next move up the crime ladder, but early into it he got caught. His cherubic face had been mentioned many times in the press, but it was during this particular arrest that the police department added "Baby Face" to his name. The press loved it and the nickname stuck.

In July 1931, Nelson was sentenced to "one year to life" for robbery and Helen and the children moved in with his mother. The following February, Nelson was again brought to court to face charges on a previous robbery, again found guilty, and again sentenced to one year to life. It looked like he would be in jail for a long time, but the prisoner had other plans.

On the day Nelson was being returned to Joliet Prison, the Gillis family went down to the train station to say goodbye to him. He was handcuffed to a corrections officer, and Helen and the others gathered a few yards away. As the train pulled out, they all waved a sad goodbye. Darkness had fallen by the time the officer and Nelson arrived at the Joliet train station and climbed into a taxi. Not far from the prison, the officer suddenly felt a poke in his ribs and looked down to see his prisoner holding a .45 automatic. Once his handcuffs were removed, Nelson ordered the driver to take them to the outskirts of Cicero, Illinois. There he forced the two men out of the car and drove off.

A week later, Father Phillip Coughlan appeared at Helen's door. A priest without a parish, Father Coughlan had floated around the fringes of the underworld for years. He'd been introduced to Nelson through some of his gangster ties and developed a strong relationship with the family. He was one of the few people Nelson trusted. Coughlan took Helen off to briefly see her husband.

Life on the run

Not long after that visit, Coughlan again showed up at the door and this time Helen was packed. She, Nelson and their son headed to Reno, Nevada, and then on to Sausalito, California. Their little daughter was left with Nelson's sisters. It was in California that Nelson met John Paul Chase, the man who became his closest friend.

When Helen suddenly became very ill and had her appendix removed, hospital staff were impressed with how devoted "Jimmie" was to his wife. To cheer her up, Nelson even had one of his sisters travel out to see them, bringing their daughter for a visit. However, after Nelson's mugshot appeared in an issue of *Detective Line-up*, the young couple thought it best to retreat to Reno again. So began the pattern of frequent relocation that would mark their domestic life.

May 1933 found them in East Chicago, Indiana, where they lived in a summer house for most of the next few months with both children. Among their regular companions there were Father Coughlan, Homer Van Meter and his girlfriend Mickey, and Tommy Carroll and his girlfriend Jean—though the home also became a focal point for many visits by other gangsters in the region that summer, including John Dillinger. It was the first meeting between Nelson and Dillinger. But it wasn't all fun and games at the house; the group also prepared for a big bank job in Grand Haven. The robbery took place in August and netted the group a large amount of money.

Next, Nelson headed up another, even more successful, bank robbery in Amery, Wisconsin. After a celebration and distribution of the booty, he, Helen, and the kids moved into a cottage at Mahtomedi, Minnesota. There they stayed until November, presenting a normal, happy family to the community. Behind the scenes, however, Nelson continued to keep in touch with Dillinger, Van Meter, and others, because in between social activities—such as visits to see relatives and vacations to Mexico—there were robberies to plan. In the early years with Helen, Nelson found it easy to slip between family life and crime. It was a job to him, one he did to provide for his wife and children. Even though he eventually brought the crimes closer and closer to his family, he never ceased to be able to change hats from vicious gangster to loving and caring husband and father.

On December 28, Illinois issued a list of the state's Top 21 public enemies. Dillinger was at the top of it. Nelson, "a convicted bank robber and escaped convict," was No. 21. For Nelson, who longed to be ranked by public opinion in the same way as Dillinger, this was a good start—at least he'd made the list. Nelson's feelings about Dillinger were part respect for, and jealousy of, the latter's notoriety. Dillinger, meanwhile—despite their working relationship—did not really care for Nelson, viewing the young man as a bit reckless, a loose cannon.

When Helen was hospitalized with anemia in San Francisco in January the next year, Nelson spent the two weeks there by her side. After her release, he drove her to Reno to recuperate and they stayed there a month. The big news on the streets was that

Dillinger and some of his gang had been captured. Nelson was anxious to return to Chicago and tried to convince Helen to wait for him in Reno. She wouldn't hear of it. Where he went, she went.

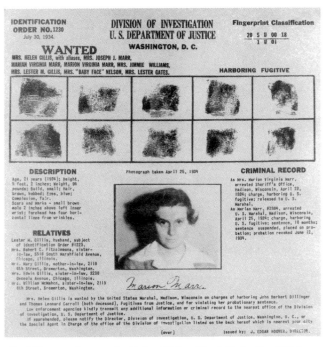

The FBI wanted poster for Helen Gillis, wife of "Baby Face" Nelson.

Back in Chicago, Nelson got down to business as usual. He, Van Meter, and Carroll had three bank robberies to plan. The only thing they lacked was more manpower. What to do?

What happened next has never been fully explained, but on March 3, 1934, Dillinger managed to escape from prison with the help of a wooden fake gun he had made himself. He also had a real one that his lawyer, Louis Piquett, had arranged to have smuggled into the jail.

Nelson had also played a large role in this and Dillinger felt begrudgingly beholden to him. After a reunion with his girlfriend, Evelyn "Billie" Frechette, Dillinger was now available for work—and Nelson and the others had their manpower problem solved.

Back to the bank

"Get your head down or I'll blow you to hell!" Nelson yelled at a bank cashier in Sioux Falls, South Dakota, on March 6. She had been slow in responding when he ordered everyone to hit the floor.

The bank was filled with customers at the time and the police had already been called. It looked like the robbers might not get away this time, but they grabbed many of the customers as a shield to make their break from the bank. In a scene that could have been right out of the movies, they forced them up onto the running boards of the car and drove away with the hostages clinging to the outside. No one dared shoot at the fleeing vehicle. One officer was shot but not killed. The gangsters netted $8,000 each from the job.

A week later, another robbery, this time in Mason City, Iowa, took place with much the same results. Nelson stood guard in the alley for this one. Inside the bank, a switchboard operator lying low on the balcony overlooking the bank floor managed to crawl away into the offices. Running to a rear window, she leaned out and saw a man in a tan overcoat on the ground below.

"Hey, mister!" she cried down to him. "Notify the police! The bank is being robbed!"

"Lady," Nelson called back up to her, revealing his machine gun. "You're telling me?"

But he was a bit spooked and didn't like the way this was going. Suddenly, he caught sight of a figure nearby and, without hesitation, fired. Racing over to the fallen man, he saw the victim was not armed.

"Stupid son of a bitch!" he swore at the bleeding man. "I thought you were a cop."

Finally the group got away, but Dillinger and another gang member were wounded. They sped to St. Paul and found a doctor to tend to their injuries.

Leaving the two behind to heal, Nelson decided to go west again with Chase, Helen, their son, and Nelson's mother in tow. While the family vacationed in Reno, Nelson and Chase busied themselves with abducting and murdering a government witness due to appear at an upcoming trial of two of Nelson's gangland friends.

Moving back to Chicago once again, the gang slowly began to regroup. Dillinger, subject of a recent police trap from which he narrowly escaped but his girlfriend Billie did not, was deeply depressed about her being in prison. His attempts to free her were for naught, which is why he was alone when the gang met a few weeks later at Louie Cernocky's Roadhouse to plan their next move—a short weekend vacation at a Wisconsin lodge Louie said would give them protection.

The gang set out for Little Bohemia in four separate cars, with Nelson and Carroll staying close together. Halfway to their destination Nelson was in an accident. No one was hurt and Nelson paid off the other driver before dropping his car off at a garage, but Helen was badly shaken. She took several swigs of whiskey from Carroll's flask to calm herself after she and Nelson climbed into Carroll's car to drive the rest of the way to the lodge. She later told her in-laws that she thought the accident had been an omen and that "right then and there, we should have turned around and headed back to Chicago."

But they drove on to Little Bohemia Lodge and what would become a key event in gangster history (see Chapter One).

Helen and Les are together again

In May 1934, Helen and Jean took the train back to Chicago after their release on probation. Helen knew without a doubt that it wouldn't be long before she was reunited with Nelson. She was not the only one confident about seeing her fugitive husband again. So were the feds, who were keeping a close eye on both her and Jean once they got to Chicago.

After shooting at Special Agent Melvin Purvis from the cabin that night at Little Bohemia, Nelson managed to escape, but later that day he had to kill one agent and wound two others to complete the getaway. He was now a heavily marked man. This, however, did not stop him from making contact with his wife. On May 31, Helen and Jean received a note that it was time for them to slip away. That evening, the four agents set up across the street from the women's apartment saw the pair leave with nothing more than their handbags. They stopped briefly to talk to Father Coughlan outside the building before walking off down the street and around the corner out of sight of the agents. Coughlan followed.

The Division of Investigation had recently held

discussions with the priest and believed he was now cooperating with them in hunting down gangsters. So, rather than blow the informant's cover, the agents stayed put—at least initially. When 15 minutes passed without Coughlan's return, they raced down to the street and around the corner after the women. Not far away they found Coughlan sitting down. He pointed to a movie theater and said he was sure they'd come out soon. Helen and Jean had indeed gone into the theater, but then soon ducked out the back where they were picked up by Nelson and Carroll. They headed north to Lake Geneva, 75 miles away, and were met there by Chase and his girlfriend.

With the heat increasing, Nelson and Helen once again left their children with relatives and went underground. Only for meetings in Chicago with Dillinger and Van Meter would Nelson surface briefly. Helen went along to many of these. The relationship between Van Meter and Nelson had grown icy since Nelson had heard that Mickey Comforti, Van Meter's girlfriend, was aiding the feds in their search for him. Only necessity kept them all together.

A bank in South Bend, Indiana, was their next target, but they needed another recruit. On Dillinger's recommendation, "Pretty Boy" Floyd was brought in to join them on the job. Van Meter had assured them of a huge payoff with this one, but it turned out to be one of those times when nothing went according to plan. A gun battle erupted at the bank, a policeman was killed, and seven innocent customers were injured. Nelson himself took a shot to the back, but his bullet-proof vest saved him. When they finally got away and counted their loot, they had just under $28,500—nowhere near what they thought they'd get. Then Floyd disappeared, taking much more than his share.

The group was angry and knew they'd have to try again. It wasn't long before they were planning the biggest job of their lives: robbing a mail train. As usual, Helen tagged along when Nelson had a midnight meeting with the others on July 15. She sat in the car, reading a magazine by flashlight, while the men talked and smoked outside. Suddenly they were interrupted by two Illinois state troopers. Gunfire was exchanged, wounding one of the troopers seriously, before the gang roared off—Helen with them—to make their escape.

With the mail train job only a week away, another meeting was called on July 21. Van Meter didn't show up. Tensions had been boiling over and Nelson lost his cool over this no-show. Dillinger promised to find Van Meter and bring him to Nelson the next night. That was the last time any of them ever saw Dillinger again. The following day he was gunned down by police as he came out of Chicago's Biograph Theater after watching a gangster film called *Manhattan Melodrama*.

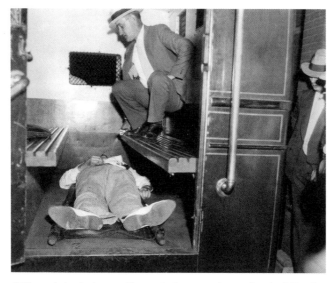

Dillinger's body in a police patrol wagon immediately following his slaying at the Biograph Theater in Chicago.

With Dillinger dead and Van Meter having vanished, the dream of the group's big score collapsed. On top of this, the feds had just named Nelson the new Public Enemy No.1—his dream achieved. He knew it was time, yet again, to get out of town.

For the next few months, he and Helen stayed on the move, hooking up from time to time with Chase. The two men were the best of friends, but Chase had recently taken up with a woman named Sally Bachman – someone Nelson didn't trust, with good reason, as it would turn out. She didn't care much for him either, because she blamed him for leading Chase into crime.

In early October 1934, Sally was arrested in San Francisco after she returned home from seeing Chase. For two weeks agents talked to her, trying to convince her to cooperate and tell them where to find him, saying that if she loved Chase this was the best thing she could do for him to keep him alive. Finally she capitulated and gave them as much information as she had. One vital piece was about a place a few hours from Chicago: she had heard Nelson say he wanted to return there for the winter.

Agents took her to the area and she eventually pinpointed the Lake Como Inn at Lake Geneva. In early November, agents questioned the owner, who feigned shock that the man he knew as "Jimmie" was the infamous gangster. He agreed to help them capture him.

A trap was laid, with government agents staking out the house for three weeks. Sure enough, on November 27, Nelson, Helen, and Chase showed up. But when he pulled in and saw an unfamiliar man on the porch, Nelson knew in an instant that something was up. The man in question was an agent. He'd heard the car and, thinking it was either the inn-keeper's wife or another agent, had left his gun inside as he went out to greet her. Nelson sped off in the direction of Barrington while the agent rushed to phone Sam Cowley, his superior in Chicago. Cowley ordered agents William Ryan and Thomas McDade to drive over to Lake Geneva immediately and be on the lookout for Nelson's car. Then Cowley himself, with another agent, Herman Hollis, headed in the same direction.

The final gunfight

It was not the first time she had been in a dangerous situation with her husband, but as the car raced along, Helen Gillis wondered if it might be the last. To reassure them both, she rested her left hand on his knee while he drove. On Lester "Baby Face" Nelson's other knee rested a .38 caliber Colt automatic.

Just seconds before, Nelson had noticed they were being followed. He could see the other vehicle gaining fast. The decision was quick. Instead of trying to outrun it, he spun his black sedan around and drove straight toward his pursuers—the two government agents, Ryan and McDade.

He raced past them and did another U-turn, coming up beside them. As the two cars drew parallel on the road, he yelled at his pursuers through his open window, "Pull over!"

Suddenly the agents spotted his accomplice in the back seat of the sedan. John Paul Chase had a gun aimed right at them. The driver of the government car floored the gas pedal. At the same moment Nelson roared at Chase, "Let 'em have it!" and shoved Helen's head below the dashboard. Both sides opened fire as Helen crouched low. The agents sped off, with the gangsters now the pursuers. The agents' only hope was to get away and lay a trap up ahead.

The plan might have worked except that Nelson didn't follow: his sedan had sustained serious damage during the exchange of gunfire. On the outskirts of Barrington, the car rapidly lost power. Worse, a second government vehicle, carrying Sam Cowley and Herman Hollis, had moved in to tail them. Nelson realized they could go no farther; he pulled over at the entrance to Barrington Park and the three leapt from the car. As Nelson and Chase barricaded themselves behind it, guns drawn and ready for the shootout they knew was coming, Helen stumbled to the ditch and hid among the reeds.

Nelson had spun his car to a stop so quickly that he caught Cowley and Hollis off guard and they went almost 120 feet past the gangsters before they were able to screech to a stop. They both began firing as they leapt from their car.

At least six bullets from Cowley's Thompson machine gun ripped into Nelson within the first few seconds, but still the latter managed to return fire. Cowley was hit twice and went down. Chase didn't even realize his friend was shot because Nelson kept reloading guns and shooting. Nelson then grabbed a .351 rifle from the back seat of the car and started to move out into the open toward the agents' car, shooting from the hip. Hollis fired and hit both of Nelson's legs, knocking him down. Still he managed to pull himself up and keep walking, adrenaline coursing through his body.

"It was just like Jimmy Cagney," a witness later said. "I never seen nothing like it. That fellow just came right a'coming at them two lawmen and they must of hit him plenty, but nothing was gonna stop that fellow."

Hollis tried to retreat, but there was nowhere to go. A bullet from Nelson's rifle ripped his head open. Nelson eased his body into the agents' vehicle and backed it up, calling twice for Helen and shouting at Chase to gather up all the weapons. As Chase began to climb into the passenger seat, Nelson said to him, "You'll have to drive. I'm shot."

Seventeen times—at least, that was the number given out by the media at the time, although later accounts put the actual number at nine. It was more than enough.

Finally, Helen ran from her hiding place and jumped into the back seat. They drove off. The Battle of Barrington was over.

She'd been through a lot with Nelson before, but this time Helen knew it was serious. "Les tried to drive but couldn't make it," Helen recounted to her family that night. "I knew it was no use trying to get a doctor. I knew as we rode that he wouldn't be my pal much longer."

At almost 5:00 p.m., they pulled up at the home of Father Coughlan's sister and asked to see the priest.

"Jimmie's been shot," Helen told him. "You have to help us."

Coughlan hurried out to the car and Nelson managed to say hello when he saw him. However, the priest would not allow them inside his sister's house for fear of involving her. He offered to help them find a safe location, though he was not sure about where that might be. He jumped in his car and instructed Chase to follow behind in the other car.

Even as he was dying, Nelson's instincts kicked in. Old friend or not, there was something about Coughlan that Nelson didn't trust that evening. He told Chase to lose Coughlan's car and, instead, directed them to the home of Ray Henderson, an underworld connection. Chase and Henderson carried the severely bleeding Nelson to a back bedroom.

"Don't leave me now," Nelson begged Chase.

Chase stayed for a short time, but when the owner of the house urged him to get rid of the car he decided that he not only wanted to ditch the car, he wanted to get out of town, fast.

Helen was left alone with her dying husband. She removed his clothes and tied a rag around the gaping abdominal wound to try to stop the bleeding. She cleaned the leg wounds and covered him with a blanket. His pain gave way to numbness as Helen held his hand and waited for the end.

"Say goodbye to Mother," he said.

Then he recited each family member's name one by one, crying when he reached his children. A few minutes later, he said, "It's getting dark, Helen. I can't see you anymore."

It was 7:35 p.m. on November 27, 1934. Baby Face Nelson, barely a week shy of his twenty-sixth birthday, was dead. Helen didn't know what to do, so she stayed with him most of the night, holding him to her. With daylight coming, Henderson helped her put the naked body in the car and they drove until they came to a cemetery. There they laid him on the grass and did not, Helen later said, throw him in a ditch as many

In 1935 Helen Gillis, widow of "Baby Face" Nelson, pleaded guilty before a federal court in San Francisco to charges of harboring her late husband.

newspapers reported. She took a red, green, and black blanket and carefully wrapped it around her husband's body because, as she later explained, "Les always hated the cold."

She then phoned the undertaker who had buried her mother and sister and asked him to take care of the body. The police were called by the undertaker and the body was picked up.

Even though federal officials claimed they never publicly stated it, the press now referred to Helen as the first female Public Enemy No. 1.

"No Mercy for Gangster's Widow," read a heading in the *New York Times*.

"'Kill Widow of Baby-Face!' U.S. orders gang hunters," proclaimed the *Chicago Herald and Examiner*.

Helen's family was frantic. Her father begged her through the press to surrender to the federal agents hunting her. "Give up rather than face government bullets," he told her. Two days after Nelson's death, on Thanksgiving evening, Helen voluntarily turned herself over to the authorities.

She eventually testified against Chase—payback for his betrayal in leaving her and Nelson that night. (Chase was finally arrested and sentenced to life imprisonment.) She served another year in prison before being released back to her children. Helen remained close to Nelson's mother until the latter's death in 1961. She never remarried and lived her later years with her son. On her death in July 1987, she was buried next to her husband in the Gillis family plot.

In a rare interview given years later, Helen expressed no regrets over the life Nelson had led her into. In fact, she insisted, she would do the same things over again if she could.

"I loved Les," she said. "When you love a guy, you love him. That's all there is to it."

Chapter Three
MOLLS ON THE RUN

Jean Delaney Crompton was one of the three gun molls arrested early on April 23, 1934, when federal agents moved in on the gangsters hiding out at Little Bohemia Lodge. She, like Helen Gillis, received probation and then quickly slipped away out of sight of the law. In Jean's case, slipping away meant returning to the arms of Tommy Carroll, a gangster on the low end of the Public Enemy list.

For Jean, hanging out with gangsters was a family trait. She and both of her sisters were involved with various members of what was always referred to as the Dillinger Gang. "Gang" was a very fluid term in the 1930s criminal world, used more by the press and law enforcement officials than by gangsters themselves. Furthermore, John Dillinger (after whom this pseudo-gang was named) was often not even in command. Frequently, the outlaws were led by Helen Gillis's husband, Lester "Baby Face" Nelson, and other high-profile members such as Alvin "Creepy" Karpis.

Jean, the middle of the three Delaney girls, was only 21 years old when she met Carroll, but she was by no means naïve. Born in Cincinnati, Ohio, in 1912, she later moved to St. Paul, Minnesota, with her family. At 19, she married Eddie Crompton, a singing waiter she'd met while working in a Chicago club. They separated a year later.

The most educated of the sisters, Jean was a voracious reader who regularly withdrew library books to read throughout her time on the run with Carroll; she left one of these borrowed books behind at Little Bohemia Lodge when she was arrested. Both her sisters had become involved with gangsters early on, but Jean avoided the temptation until her separation from Crompton. St. Paul was a focal point in the early 1930s for criminal activity and the women were frequently in the presence of well-known gangsters such as Alvin Karpis and the Barker brothers Arthur and Fred (sons of the famous "Ma" Barker). It was through these connections that Jean met Carroll, eleven years her senior. He was a veteran bank robber, who had done at least three jobs with the Barker-Karpis ensemble. Although Jean was bright, she seemed content to let Carroll dominate her from the start. He had a history of abusing other women before Jean, and he was not above hitting her if she did not comply with his orders or asked too many questions about his criminal activities.

While Carroll escaped that day at Little Bohemia, Jean ended up in jail and eventually pleading guilty to harboring a federal fugitive. She received extra care and treatment during her time in custody because she was pregnant. Initially Jean told authorities her name was Ann Southern (after an actress of the day). When she was visited at the jail by her older sister, Helen "Babe" Reilly, the *Wisconsin State Journal* reported:

"The blonde Ann and her attractive brunette sister, clad in a neat blue suit with white trimmings, embraced, wept a bit and talked about family affairs when the two met for the first time since the three girls were deserted by fleeing gangsters."

Babe, who had endured a number of unflattering portrayals in the media showing her to be the pathetic and unhappy older sister, confronted the press after she visited Jean.

"If you put in any more sob stuff about me, I'll tear your old paper in two," she told them.

Although promising to go straight, Jean moved in with Helen Gillis right after their release, and the two escaped police surveillance on May 31, 1934. Her reunion with Carroll was bittersweet. At some point in the next week, Jean lost her baby, through abortion or miscarriage (she'd had a miscarriage during her brief marriage). She also dyed her blonde hair black. She later said she did so not to disguise herself but because she was tired of blonde hair and hated being called Mae West (after the actress) in jail.

On June 7, Carroll drove Jean to see her mother in St. Paul. They stopped in Waterloo, Iowa, to get gas and have the oil checked. They also did some shopping for Jean, including a new dress (which she changed into immediately) and glasses. After the car was attended to, they went to a nearby bar on Lafayette Street to grab a beer. What they didn't know was that an alert station attendant had become suspicious when he'd opened the hood of the car and noticed several out-of-state license plates hidden there. He called the police.

By the time the couple returned to the car, officers were waiting for them. "We stepped up and identified ourselves," Detective Emil Steffen told the *Chicago Tribune*. "He tried to reach for a gun. [Sheriff P.E.] Walker jumped for him and grappled with him. That gave me a chance to draw my gun. I plugged him at least once . . . and the guy made a break. By that time Walker had a chance to get out his gun and he opened up as the man tried to get away."

This was all done with the officers also holding on to Jean, who was kicking, screaming, crying, and trying to get away. She watched as her lover took five bullets.

Badly wounded, Carroll was removed to hospital while Jean was taken to jail, where she was interviewed by a reporter.

"Tell him I still love him," Jean told the reporter. "Tell him not to die."

"Tell her I'm all right," Carroll reportedly told the doctor at the hospital.

Unfortunately, he wasn't, and he died not long after being administered last rights by a priest. Jean fainted when she heard the news. Later, viewing Carroll's body at the morgue, she sobbed. And still she resolutely refused to give up any information to the police about Carroll's business and colleagues.

Jean's probation was revoked for being captured with Carroll and she was ordered to prison for a year. During that time, she took typing classes and attended Catholic Mass, determined to start a fresh life for herself after her release, which came on March 31, 1935. In December of that year Jean was granted a divorce from Edward Crompton on the grounds of abandonment. With that, she picked up the pieces of her life and slipped quietly into obscurity.

Sisters in crime

It was unusual, to say the least, that all three Delaney sisters ended up in love with gangsters. They were all young, beautiful, and bold, and stood by their men even when they were no longer with them.

The Delaney girls' mother blamed their paths to trouble on her oldest daughter Babe and her association with, and subsequent marriage to, Pat Reilly. She felt Reilly led her daughter down the path to ruin. Helen "Babe" Delaney and Reilly were teenagers when they married and, in truth, it was likely Babe who introduced Reilly to the criminal life in St. Paul —not the other way around.

Babe was the only one of the three sisters to avoid prison. However, she stood by the other two at all their trials and releases. She and Reilly had a son whom she struggled to support after she left her husband in 1933. Babe's mother was delighted to see Reilly behind bars after his arrest in June 1934 for harboring a criminal, but Babe herself did not feel the same hatred for him. Federal agents discovered this when they put her under arrest at the same time as they revoked her sister Jean's probation. Babe was held in custody and questioned for five days, but refused to "be a stool pigeon" and turn Reilly in for the reward money.

Delores, the youngest—and likely most hardened —of the Delaney sisters fell in love with Canadian-born Alvin Karpis when she was only seventeen years old. Said a *New York Times* article in 1936:

> *"'Ma' Barker [mother of the Barker brothers, one of whom she would die beside in a 1935 police shootout] knew Delores Delaney, a pretty St. Paul girl, and was anxious to have Karpis, her 'pet,' make her acquaintance. So not long afterward Dolores and Karpis met at Harry Sawyer's saloon on Wabasha Street in St. Paul."*

The dawning of 1935 found Karpis, 25, at the top of the charts: Public Enemy No. 1. The previous three to be top of the list had all died in 1934 (John Dillinger, "Pretty Boy" Floyd, and "Baby Face" Nelson). By this time, Delores was pregnant. Karpis moved her to Miami and found a house for her there during the late stages of her pregnancy. Karpis also hired a surgeon to deliver the baby, saying, "We have plenty of dough, and we want the best for the little girl [Delores]."

Like most expectant mothers, Delores busied herself making baby clothes as the birth approached. Unlike most expectant mothers, however, she had the police after her and the baby's father. When Ma Barker and her son Fred were killed by the police on January 16, Karpis told Delores to pack up quickly because they were heading to Atlantic City, New Jersey. She did as she was asked and tucked all the baby clothes she'd made into several suitcases. While Karpis and an associate, Harry Campbell, made the trip up the Eastern seaboard by car, the very pregnant Delores and a friend were left to take

A prison photograph of "Moll" Delores Delaney, girlfriend of gangster Al Karpis.

the train. Karpis met them on arrival and they quickly got rooms at the Danmore Hotel.

Meanwhile, the Atlantic City police had already received a tip from Florida to be on the lookout for Karpis's car. Officers scoured garages in the area until they located the vehicle and traced its occupants to the hotel. It was 4:00 a.m. on January 20 when six heavily armed policemen approached the hotel. Three stayed downstairs while the others moved in on Karpis's hotel room. They noticed the door to his room was slightly ajar and nudged it open slowly. Karpis was waiting for them, sitting in an armchair holding a machine gun.

As he saw Karpis, one of the officers shouted, "Stick 'em up!"

"Stick 'em up yourself, copper!" came the reply and the shooting started. In the ensuing battle, a bullet from one of the guns hit Delores in the leg, but not seriously. In the mayhem, Karpis and Campbell managed to escape from the building. When they saw their own car guarded, they simply stole another one. They circled the hotel twice hoping to rescue the women, but finally had to leave. They had their freedom, but the women did not.

Delores was taken into custody after a trip to the hospital to have her leg wound treated. A few days later she gave birth to a baby boy, whom she gave to Karpis's parents to raise. At that point, the federal officials guarding her agreed to release the suitcases full of baby clothes that she'd brought with her from Florida. Delores was eventually transferred to Miami to stand trial. She pleaded guilty to harboring a fugitive, but refused to give officials any information in exchange for a lighter sentence. In the end she received a five-year prison term, the longest sentence given to any moll under the harboring law.

Karpis was finally tracked down and arrested in 1936 and received a lengthy jail sentence. Of the four men in the 1930s to be declared Public Enemy No. 1, Karpis was the only one not to meet a violent end. He lived out a full life, passing away in Spain in 1979.

Delores was released from prison November 30, 1938, and within a couple of years the woman J. Edgar Hoover called a "silly little moll" had slipped from view.

Marie "Mickey" Comforti

And the last of the three women arrested at Little Bohemia? She was Marie "Mickey" Comforti—the one who had been clutching her little terrier that day at Little Bohemia in April 1934 when the federal agents moved in to arrest those whom they hoped were members of Dillinger's gang.

Mickey had every intention of staying on the right side of the law once she emerged from prison. As with Helen Gillis and Jean Delaney Crompton, federal agents were keeping a close surveillance on her. Unluckily for her, the other two slipped past the federal net for a while to freedom. That left her as the only one to follow.

"When the judge let me go I came to Chicago and tried to live an honest life," the 21-year-old told the *Chicago Daily Tribune*. "I was waitress in a restaurant and I clerked in a 10 cent store. If the agents hadn't persecuted me I'd be a good girl now. They took me on long rides, trying to trap me into telling them about "Baby Face" Nelson. They even made me go out and talk to Nelson's mother. I got so afraid some of the boys would see me with the agents and think I was a squealer. So I went back to Homer Van Meter."

Van Meter was a long-time Dillinger associate. He was unfaithful to Mickey (having another girlfriend at the same time) and frequently left her for long periods of time. They were together in Chicago, however, leading up to August 23, 1934 —the day Van Meter was gunned down by police in a barrage of bullets. Rumors abounded that he had been set up by the underworld because he'd become unstable and they were afraid of what he might say if caught. Two days after his death, Mickey surrendered. She became a witness for the prosecution against those harboring Van Meter, but any favorable treatment she might have received because of that was nullified when she began publicly defaming federal agent Samuel Cowley, after he was shot dead a few months later by "Baby Face" Nelson in Barrington, Illinois. Mickey declared she wasn't sorry Cowley was dead because he had tortured her.

"He chained me to a chair, and every few minutes he would ask, 'Where is Nelson?'" Mickey told the press. "Every time I said I didn't know, he slapped me and punched me."

Despite testifying, Mickey was still sent to prison for harboring Van Meter. The man had never treated her well, yet she remained loyal to him and only had good things to say about being a gangster's woman.

"He was a fine fellow and I loved him," she told newsmen. "He was good to me and gave me things —a radio set and a dog. The dog was his last gift and the [sheriff] at Eagle River kept it for himself, although I wrote asking him for it several times."

Once out of the rough and tumble of underworld life, Mickey—like the Delaney girls—drifted into peace and obscurity.

Evelyn "Billie" Frechette

The one person conspicuously absent from the list of the gangsters' women arrested at Little Bohemia Lodge was John Dillinger's girlfriend Evelyn "Billie" Frechette. She most certainly would have been there with the others if she had not already been in jail.

"Only one big thing ever happened to me in my life," Billie said in a five-part piece she wrote from jail for the *Chicago Herald and Examiner* in August 1934. "Nothing much happened before that," she said, "and I don't expect much from now on—except maybe a lot more grief. The one big thing that happened to me was that I fell in love with John Dillinger."

Mary Evelyn Frechette was born in 1907. Her father was French and her mother, in her own words, was "half French and half Indian". Evelyn was First Nation and a member of the Menominee Tribe of Wisconsin. "I'm proud of my Indian blood. My tribe is a good tribe and my people are good people," she wrote. She was raised on the tribe's reservation until she was thirteen and then spent the next three years at a boarding school for Aboriginals in Flandreau, South Dakota.

By the time she was eighteen, she had graduated and was living in Chicago with her sister Frances. She found work where she could—housemaid, nurse, or waitress. The Depression was in full swing and jobs were hard to come by. Her sister was part of a group called "The Indian Players." Wearing feathers and beads and with painted faces, they put on plays that included a lot of the traditional dances they had performed on the reservation back home. Evelyn sometimes put on a costume and danced for them in the chorus.

She had turned into a beautiful woman, 5 feet 3 inches tall with a round face, dark hair and black, haunting eyes. She found Chicago liberating and explored her sexual freedom by dating a number of men. An unwanted pregnancy found her at the Beulah Home for Unmarried Women under the care of Reverend Edward Brooks.

On a cold February day in 1928, Evelyn gave birth to a baby boy, Billie, named after her father, William, who had died when she was eight years old. The baby was born with congenital syphilis which left him severely disabled. Evelyn, unable to care for him, left him with Reverend Brooks and went home to the Menominee reservation to live with her mother. When she returned to Chicago late in 1928 and enquired as to the health of her son, she was devastated to learn that he had died when he was three months old. It was around this time that Evelyn began

Evelyn "Billie" Frechette, lover of John Dillinger, who went on the run with him.

to call herself "Billie" and she was always known by this name thereafter.

Billie later admitted she was always attracted to bad boys and on August 2, 1932, she and Patricia Young married Welton Spark and Arthur Cherrington respectively at the county jail prior to the men's incarceration at Leavenworth, Kansas. Billie had not known Spark long but was living with him at the time of his arrest.

"I wasn't really in love with him," she later wrote, "but I was lonesome."

Billie forgot about Spark relatively quickly, but it was her marriage to him that eventually stopped her from being able to marry John Dillinger as she so longed to do.

Dillinger was born June 22, 1903 and crime was always his life. He married Beryl Hovious at nineteen, though she divorced him only five years later. His trouble with the law led him to join the Navy, but he ended up deserting a few months later. His first prison time was at the Indiana Reformatory at Pendleton, where he met a number of seasoned criminals who later became the core of his gang. Dillinger learned a great deal from them by the time of his parole in May 1933 and lost no time in returning to crime.

Billie and Pat Cherrington had supported

themselves in Chicago since their husbands had gone to jail. According to Ellen Paulsen in *Don't Call Us Molls*, they both waived the home relief available to them as wives of federal convicts. Pat and her sister Opal Long mixed in the same circles as Billie and they were all a part of each other's lives, spending their nights at the many clubs in Chicago. It was at one of these places that John Dillinger walked into Billie's life that summer, introduced to her as Jack Harris.

"There was something in those eyes that I will never forget," Billie later told *True Confessions* magazine. "They were piercing and electric, yet there was an amused carefree twinkle in them too. They met my eyes and held me hypnotized for an instant."

The feelings were reciprocated by Dillinger. While Billie was the target of a great deal of prejudice on account of her heritage, Dillinger found her cultural and Roman Catholic background fascinating. They were inseparable.

Once out of jail, Dillinger and his gang had quickly begun robbing banks. The men and their girlfriends often lived together, moving as the law necessitated. Especially close to Billie and Dillinger were Harry Pierpont/Mary Kinder and Harry Copeland/Pat Cherrington. Mary and Billie both liked to drink a lot, which worried both their partners. The men drank very little in order to keep their heads clear.

Billie was never actively involved with the crimes, as Bonnie may have been with Clyde, nor did she load guns during the crimes as Helen did for "Baby Face" Nelson. However, she did at times drive the getaway car when she and Dillinger were in trouble.

Their first narrow escape from the law was in November 1933, when Dillinger had to go to a doctor for treatment of ringworm. Set up by an informant, Dillinger became suspicious of men walking toward him as he headed for the doctor's office and leaped for the car with Billie inside. As he roared away he pointed his gun out the window and fired on the pursuing vehicles. It was assumed the woman riding with him had done the shooting and it was the first time that Billie was mentioned with Dillinger, although under the name of Billie Spark. Somehow they escaped.

On December 19 Dillinger and Billie arrived in Daytona Beach, Florida. It was a holiday for all as the gang joined them. They purchased vast amounts of clothes and jewelry and saw all the sights but kept a relatively low profile, trying not to draw attention to themselves. Billie acquired a diamond ring and a platinum watch studded with diamonds, and Dillinger put his Essex Terraplane car into her name. After Christmas she used it to go to the reservation to see her family. He also gave her thousands of dollars to buy things for both the Dillinger family in Indiana and her own family. There was some talk that the two had a fight and that he physically abused her, but this was always vehemently denied by both her family and the other women in the gang.

Billie had an accident in the car on her way back to Chicago and barely made it to Milwaukee, where she visited a friend and acquired a new car. While she was away Dillinger had been involved in a robbery where a police officer was killed, the first and only murder ever attributed to him. She met up with him not long after and the two of them drove to Tucson, Arizona, stopping in St. Louis to buy a faster car. By January 23 the gang had all found their way to Tucson. They were a close-knit group and fond of each other, but their reunion was to be short-lived.

A fire broke out in their hotel and some of the group feared that the flames would set off the ammunition they had in their bags, so they paid a fireman to bring the bags out. The weight of them made him suspicious and on reading a detective magazine later, he recognized one of the gang in a photo. He contacted the authorities and within a short period of time they were all under arrest, including Billie, although she was "Ann Martin" through the entire process. No one knew her real name. On January 27, 1934, Opal Long and Ann Martin were released from custody.

Dillinger was not as lucky. Indiana took him for the murder charges and Ohio claimed the other men.

Billie and Opal were free but completely broke; all their jewelry, clothes, and cash had been confiscated by the authorities. Somehow they reached Kansas City, where Opal had relatives, but ultimately Billie found her way back to Chicago and lived with her sister on money coming from Dillinger's lawyer, Louis Piquett.

What happened next and how much of a role Billie played is uncertain. Dillinger was quite the celebrity and photos of him relaxing with officials in Crown Point County Jail came back to haunt them later on. Billie visited Dillinger at the prison with Piquett on February 16. She was searched and watched, but how much she was able to give Dillinger in terms of information, money, or more is not known. While she was talking to him the guards noted she threw in a bunch of numbers between the words and she was warned to stop. On March 3, with the help of both a fake gun and, it was later shown, a real one, her lover broke out of jail. Because he then stole the Sheriff's car and drove it across state lines, he became a federal fugitive.

Public officials loved being seen with Dillinger. Here Sheriff Lillian Holley (left) and Lake County prosecutor Robert Estill (center) pose with the gangster. Photos such as this contributed to both of them losing their jobs after his escape.

Dillinger and Billie were together again, but for a short time and in precarious circumstances. It was decided that Billie would stay temporarily in Detroit with Opal Long. Dillinger went to St. Paul to find two old friends he trusted, Homer Van Meter and

John "Red" Hamilton, and then joined Tommy Carroll, Eddie Green, and "Baby Face" Nelson to form a new gang. On March 6 he committed his first robbery with his new cohorts.

During a bank robbery March 13, Dillinger was wounded in the shoulder, although not seriously. A few days later he sent Billie to give some money to Piquett and then on to Mooresville, Indiana with money for his father. She became his go-between with Piquett.

The landlady of the Lexington Avenue apartment where they were now staying in St. Paul was becoming suspicious of the secrecy and lavish spending of her new tenants, Mr. and Mrs. Carl Hellman, and passed on her concerns to the post master, who immediately phoned the police. On the morning of March 31 while the two were still in bed, there was a knock on the door. Billie, thinking it was one of their friends, answered it to find an agent asking to speak to Mr. Carl Hellman. It took her a second to comprehend the situation but she answered quickly, saying her husband was not home and she'd let them in as soon as she was dressed.

By the time she closed the door and put the chain across, Dillinger was already pulling on his clothes and telling her to pack one suitcase while he grabbed his machine gun and stalled for time, hoping one of his friends would come to the rescue. Homer Van Meter just happened to come into the building at the time but quickly saw what was happening and escaped amid a flurry of bullets, distracting the agents.

Dillinger, hearing the shots and figuring it was his cue, fired volleys of bullets through the front door while Billie got out into the hallway with their heavy suitcase and went down the back stairway. She dragged it to the garage, where she got their car and drove it to a spot behind the building as Dillinger had instructed. He was able to fire his way to the car but not without being shot in the leg, which rendered him unable to drive.

They roared away, Billie at the wheel, and parked near to Eddie Green's house. She was petrified, as she described in her piece in the *Chicago Herald and Examiner*.

"For a minute I thought I couldn't get up off the seat of the car," she wrote. "I felt sure that if I got out and started down the street I'd get a bullet in my back before I got two feet away."

Billie arrived at Green's house begging for help. He in turn went to Pat Reilly to find a doctor while Billie waited, terrified, in the car with Dillinger. After medical attention on his knee, they spent the next three days at the home of the doctor's nurse until Dillinger could walk around again and then they went to the one place no one would suspect because it was so obvious—the home of Dillinger's father in Mooresville, Indiana. They spent a wonderful couple of days there on the farm, much as Bonnie and Clyde did with their families near the end. They shared meals and games and took photos. Dillinger's family loved Billie and wanted to see the two married.

Indeed, throughout much of their time together Dillinger gave Billie money for lawyers toward her attempts to end her marriage to Spark. She had recently gone to another one in order to try to finalize her divorce. She and Dillinger were desperate to be married. He mentioned again to his father that he wanted to go away with Billie somewhere and start over. It was a pipe dream, of course. They were both going to get caught sooner or later. For Billie it would be the former.

After the short family respite the couple went to Chicago, where they had been assured that an associate, Larry Streng, would find a hideout for them. Billie had made an appointment for her and Dillinger to meet with Streng at the Austin-State Tavern Monday April 9. However, he had accidentally given

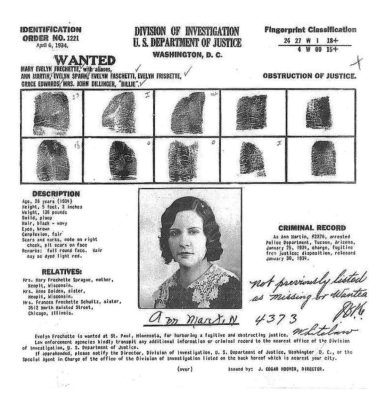

Billie Frechette's FBI wanted poster.

information on this meeting to an informant and Streng was arrested only a few minutes before their arrival.

Dillinger stayed in the car down the street while Billie went ahead into the tavern. He then watched in horror as his lover was delivered into the arms of Agent Melvin Purvis, the man in charge of the task force to bring in Dillinger and his gang. There was nothing he could do.

Authorities hoped to break Billie for information, but she was made of stronger stuff than they anticipated. She was held without charges or representation for three days, the last two deprived of sleep or food by the two agents who took over her interrogation. She would later accuse one of them of physical abuse as well (the press reported her as saying she had her hair pulled, her stomach kicked, and her face slapped). When Louis Piquett discovered Billie had been held incommunicado for three days he brought it to the attention of the press, and Melvin Purvis was at last forced to officially announce her arrest. Dillinger was incensed when he heard about her physical abuse and only the restraint of his friends stopped him from taking action against the agent responsible.

A warrant was issued April 12 to return Billie to St. Paul to face charges of harboring Dillinger at the Lexington Avenue apartment. The next day bail was set at $60,000 on additional charges of helping him escape from that apartment.

Dillinger was beside himself and explored a number of options to see if he could help her escape. Billie, for her part, was sending him messages not to try anything because she was terrified he would be killed in the attempt. She almost escaped without his help. While in court with her lawyers on May 15 she quietly slipped out with the jurors at lunch and made it as far as the front door before being caught.

During her trial Billie admitted she knew Dillinger was a bank robber. "I loved him just the same," she said. In a last-ditch effort, Piquett made a futile attempt to say that Billie was innocent because she had done what she did out of love for Dillinger and that made her not culpable of harboring.

The next day, May 23—the day that Bonnie and Clyde were killed in an ambush—Billie was found guilty and sentenced to two years in prison plus a $1,000 fine.

Dillinger was depressed for some time and never stopped looking for a way to get Billie out of prison, telling Piquett he would not be happy until he saw her again. He did, however, find a new girlfriend eventually. Rita "Polly" Hamilton Keele looked a lot like a younger version of Billie. She accompanied him and Anna Sage (who had set up Dillinger to be ambushed) to see a movie on the night of July 23 at the Biograph Theatre. After watching the gangster movie *Manhattan Melodrama* Polly slipped into the shadows as the gunfire started and Dillinger met his death.

Shortly after Billie went to prison, her mother was hit by a car and died. She was not allowed to attend the funeral. She had lost Dillinger and her mother in the same month. During her time in jail, Billie wrote a booklet warning the young against crime and later sold copies of it for 25 cents. After two years at the federal prison in Milan, Michigan, she was finally released January 30, 1936.

Many family members of criminals from that era took shows called "Crime Does Not Pay" on the road. They were paid well for the period to do this. The Depression was still in its latter stages and many of them had lost their jobs and status just by being affiliated with the gangsters. These shows were a way of survival and also perhaps a way to pay back for some of the damage done by their criminal relatives. Billie joined one of the shows, even posing with a wax image of a dead Dillinger, and continued with them until 1941, when she went back home to the Menominee reservation. She married twice more. Her first husband died and her final marriage, at 58, was to an older man, Arthur Tic, who apparently treated her very well until her death from cancer in 1969.

"I always figured that what he did was one thing and what he was another," Evelyn "Billie" Frechette wrote in the newspaper about Dillinger. "I was in love with what he was. Oh, maybe I was wrong, but you can't argue yourself out of falling in love!"

Chapter Four

THE RIDE OF THEIR LIVES: VI MATHIS AND VERNE MILLER

It was just another summer day for the 21-year-old at the carnival concession stand in St. Paul. Vi Mathis, a beautiful and outgoing young woman, had recently moved to Minnesota from South Dakota to be close to her parents or, more specifically, her daughter. Vi's parents were raising her four-year-old child on a dairy farm in Brainerd. On this hot day in 1926, the young woman—always up for adventure—had no idea she would soon be on a wild ride herself.

Born in Leola, South Dakota, in May 1905, Vivian Gibson was a good student and very popular. She was also attracted to dangerous young men and the first serious one came along when she was only sixteen. His name was Stanley Mathis and he was 22 when he wandered onto the Gibson farm looking for work. It didn't take long for him and Vivian to hook up. Her parents were not happy about it, but the two married in October 1921. Stanley opened a shop in Eureka and came home on weekends to his wife, who continued to live with her parents in Leola.

Early that December, Vivian and some girlfriends decided to head out for a little fun. They dressed up as men and went downtown. Their prank got them a lot of laughs, though one person wasn't amused. Clarence Berry had been Leola's night watchman for only a few months. It wasn't much of a job—just checking on stores and seeing that drunks got home—but he took it seriously, carrying a billy club, a gun and a flashlight. When he came across Vivian and her friends in the late evening, he wanted to know why they were out at that hour and why they were disguised. He shooed them home. Not only did they pay no attention, but they laughed at him. This infuriated him and he swore at them, calling them "God damn little idiots."

When Stanley got home that weekend and heard the story, he, Vivian, and two friends decided to repeat the charade. This time everyone got into the act, with the women dressing as men again, and the men dressing as women. It was all good fun, but eventually the other couple headed home, leaving Stanley and Vivian hanging out downtown. Whether Stanley was actually itching for a confrontation with the night watchman or not isn't known, but he got one.

Berry came across the couple sitting on a bench, exchanged a few words with them, and then tried to leave. At that point, Stanley stood up and confronted him. Shouting broke out and then suddenly shots were fired. Both men were wounded. Berry crawled to a neighbor and was taken to hospital, where he died hours later. Stanley, hit in the thigh, eventually made it home. The next morning, police arrived at the farm and arrested him for murder. Because he was known to be moody and short-tempered, it seemed an open and shut case. Furthermore, Berry had managed to tell his story before he died. Stanley, he said, had deliberately followed him down the street, pulled a .25 automatic, and shot him twice.

The case had one unexpected twist before it was over, though. Vivian, then visibly pregnant, took the stand at the trial and gave a very different account of events. Berry swore at her, she said, and when Stanley defended her, Berry pulled out a gun, and shot him in the leg. It was then she, not Stanley, who shot back at Berry to protect her husband. No one believed her —the jury still found Stanley guilty and sentenced him to life in prison—but everyone voiced their admiration for the bravery that this very young pregnant woman had shown in testifying for her husband

Vivian spent the next few years working at numerous jobs to help support her daughter, who continued to live on the farm. Although she kept up the contact with Stanley for some time, in 1926 she sent a letter to the warden of the penitentiary stating she had obtained a divorce. When her parents moved to Brainerd, Vi (as she was by then known) moved as well.

That summer day at the carnival, everything was going well until Vi suddenly found herself in a heated argument with a customer. Before she knew what was happening, he'd knocked her to the ground. Out of the gathering crowd rushed another man to her rescue. His name was Verne Miller. He helped Vi to her feet and in no time the two developed a relationship.

Verne Miller's past

Vernon Clate Miller was born in South Dakota, Iowa, most likely on August 25, 1896 (although he variously gave 1891 or 1895 as birthdates, too). His parents divorced when he was young and Verne was sent to live with his uncle and aunt and their thirteen children. He was a likeable, easy-going child who went as far as Grade Four before leaving behind both education and his uncle's farm to follow the county fair circuit. There he became a parachute jumper, dropping from hot air balloons.

His adventurous streak didn't stop there. He also did a short stint with the state National Guard in North Dakota when he was seventeen, convincing the recruiters he was 21 and old enough to join up. A second stint with them ended in February 1917, just weeks before the United States Congress declared war on Germany. Knowing he would be called to war soon, Verne decided to get married and six weeks later was once again in the army. Through some bureaucratic bungling, he did not make his way to Europe to fight until April 1918, but when he got there he lost no time in distinguishing himself. He was awarded two medals of honor and nominated as an officer even though the war ended before his post was instituted. He later claimed to have also been awarded the French Croix de Guerre for bravery, but it's not clear if this was true.

Verne Miller's FBI wanted poster.

several gambling casinos with a partner from the New Jersey Mob.

It was during their frequent business trips to New York that Verne met Louis "Lepke" Buchalter and the two became close friends. Buchalter was physically a small, quiet man, but he was also the most powerful figure in labour racketeering on the East Coast. His wife became close to Vi and the couples often spent time together.

With things having settled down a little, Verne and Vi returned in early 1930 to St. Paul, America's underworld Mecca at the time because it was a city filled with corruption. Joining the gang of Tommy Holden and Francis Keating, Verne took part in a number of robberies and other crimes that gave him and Vi a good, stable life—as good and stable as a gangster's life could be, that is. Every Thanksgiving they went to her parents' farm, inviting along many of their friends. Vi's father was especially close to Verne. He thought that Verne and his friends were all businessmen—and why would he think otherwise? How could he know, for example, that in 1930, Verne was responsible for the machine-gun fire that ripped through the Manning Hotel near Fox Lake, Illinois, leaving three gangsters dead and many others wounded? Or that the 1932 bank robbery of the Third

Northwestern National Bank in Minneapolis, which resulted in the deaths of two policemen and a bystander, was the work of Verne, Alvin "Creepy" Karpis, and the Barker Brothers?

In April 1933, Verne and Vi rented a house in an upscale neighborhood of Kansas City and, with life so peaceful, Vi decided to bring her daughter home from her parents to live with them. The next few months were very happy for the family. It all lasted a remarkably short time.

Frank "Jelly" Nash, a long-time underworld friend of Verne's, got careless about being seen in public and on June 16 was nabbed by federal agents. Word quickly reached a few of Nash's friends who began scheming to free him. The plan was hatched by Richard Tallman Galatas, Herbert Farmer, "Doc" Louis Stacci, and Frank B. Mulloy. Verne was brought aboard to lead the rescue. He asked around for help and, in the end, enlisted Charles "Pretty Boy" Floyd and Adam Richetti.

Nash was en route to prison by train when it pulled into Kansas City's Union Station on the morning of Saturday, June 17, 1933. Accompanying Nash were McAlester, Oklahoma Police Chief Otto Reed, and Division of Investigation (DOI) agents Frank Smith and Joe Lackey. The party was met at the station by two Kansas City police officers, Detective William

Grooms and Frank Hermanson, plus two agents from the DOI Kansas City bureau, Reed Vetterli and Ray Caffrey. This group of seven men had Nash under tight guard as they left the station at 7:15 a.m. and headed towards two waiting cars. Four of them openly carried guns, all .38s. Lackey had a 12 gauge pump action shotgun and Reed had a 16 gauge shotgun with some unusual features. Somewhere along the way Lackey and Reed accidentally got the other's gun, with fatal results.

Police Chief Reed and Agents Lackey and Smith got into the back seat of one of the cars, Lackey preventing Nash from climbing in there too, saying, "No, you ride up front so we can all keep an eye on you." Agent Caffrey walked around the car, intending to get into the driver's seat while the other three agents stood by waiting to get into the second car.

Suddenly, from out of nowhere, Floyd was there yelling, "Up! Up! Put 'em up!"

Lackey, who as a federal agent did not carry a gun, had armed himself that morning with a shotgun but by mistake took Reed's 16-gauge sawed-off shotgun, a weapon with which he was unfamiliar. In addition the normal shells had been replaced with ones filled with very powerful ball bearings. When he heard Floyd's shout, Lackey tried to raise his gun, but it accidentally discharged, blowing off part of Nash's head. At the same instant, a ball bearing went through the windshield, hitting Caffrey as he stepped in front of the car. He died soon after.

Lackey reloaded another shell into the gun and fired, this time striking and killing Detective Hermanson outside the car. Verne and Floyd opened fire, killing Reed. An autopsy on Reed later found both machine gun bullets and a .38-caliber slug in his body (the only .38-caliber weapons at the shooting were carried by detectives Hermanson and Grooms). Grooms was also killed in the crossfire. Agent Vetterli was wounded, but managed to crawl to safety, and Agent Smith ducked down in the back seat and played dead, escaping unharmed. The man who (albeit accidentally) started the killing, Lackey, was hit several times in the back and left permanently crippled.

The three gangsters fled in a dark-colored Chevrolet. The shooting was over in 30 seconds, but the effects lasted much longer. The Kansas City Massacre, as the incident came to be called, did more to help the future Federal Bureau of Investigation get the power to fight gangsters than did any other single event to that time. The tremendous public outrage over the deaths prompted sweeping changes. In 1934, Congress passed a crime bill allowing agents, for the first time, to arrest people across state lines. It also gave federal agents the authority to carry firearms. All they had to do now was learn how to shoot them! The Bureau of Investigation, headed by J. Edgar Hoover, put out a heavily sanitized version of the massacre in which all the dead officers were killed by the gunmen.

It was never determined whether Verne was helped by Floyd alone or by Richetti as well, or if indeed two other individuals were with Verne that day instead, but the one fact everyone agreed on was that the Kansas City Massacre had been led by Verne. He later told a friend that Richetti was too hung-over from a drinking binge the night before to accompany them and that he and Floyd alone were at the station. Floyd was gunned down a year later by Melvin Purvis and other agents from the DOI. And Richetti, after being captured and tortured by agents trying to get a confession from him, wound up going to the electric chair for the murder of Officer Hermanson. He may have been no angel, but Richetti maintained his innocence for that shooting to the end. In another twist Floyd later also denied he took any part in the Kansas City Massacre. The only known truth from that day is that Nash and four other men were killed.

The net closes in

Following the Kansas City Massacre, the heat was on Verne. He and Vi went their separate ways for a while, with Vi spending the month of July traveling on the East Coast with Louis Buchalter's wife. Federal agents were on their trail most of the time. Verne expected the furore to die down within a few months after the killings. He couldn't have been more wrong. Gangsters throughout the country were quick to distance themselves from the massacre. Even Bonnie Parker made the point in one of her poems that she and Clyde had not taken part in it.

Vi, who couldn't stand being parted for too long from her "Sugar," checked into a hotel in Newark, New York, and made arrangements to meet up with him. By this time, agents had tracked her down and were sure they were closing in on their man. They forgot that the woman they were dealing with had been connected with crimes and criminals long enough to know she was being tailed.

One day, Vi complained of a toothache and phoned for a dentist to come to her hotel. The dentist recommended that she return with him to his office. The "dentist" was either Verne or an associate, but by the time the agents realized they had been hoodwinked, the couple was gone. The near-capture made Verne and Vi realize they would have to part again temporarily. Verne set about organizing a new identity and Vi went to Chicago to settle down and wait for him. She contacted an old friend there, Martha "Bobbie" Moore, to help her out.

Bobbie and Jack Harris, a small-time hood in Chicago, had known Verne and Vi in the past. In the fall of 1931, Harris went on a business trip to New York and never returned. Word got back to Bobbie that she was to assume she was a widow and it was accepted (though never proven) that Verne had killed Harris because he'd beaten Bobbie on numerous occasions. Whatever the reason for Harris's disappearance, Bobbie was very grateful to have him gone, so when Vi phoned her for help, Bobbie readily gave it. In August 1933, Vi moved in with her at the Sherone Apartments, eventually acquiring her own suite under the name of Mrs. Clara Hayes.

Meanwhile, with the fallout from the Kansas City shootings still fresh in every mind, Verne was finding all the old doors closed to him in his quest for help from the underworld. He decided he had little choice but to make a complete break and move to Europe. However, there was no way he would go without Vi, and he headed to Chicago to pick her up.

This was just what federal agents were counting

on. Weeks before, they had bugged Bobbie Moore's phone and rented an apartment on the same floor as Vi. There was one small wrinkle. Their photos of Verne were so grainy they couldn't be sure of recognizing him if he did show up at Vi's building. They needed someone who could positively identify him. The solution to the problem was solved by two people. Doris Rogers, secretary to Melvin Purvis of the DOI, had grown up in Huron, South Dakota, when Verne had been sheriff there and she remembered him well. ("I was the only woman attaché of the department of justice who ever went out on the firing line with the Chicago G-men," she later wrote [under her married name, Doris Lockerman] in 1935 in the *Chicago Daily Tribune*. "Had Melvin Purvis been in town at the time, I would have missed my most thrilling adventure. When he returned from Washington after the fray, he was hopping mad to find that the agents had taken a woman employee on a raid.")

The other person recruited was Chicago Special Agent Ed Notesteen, who knew Verne by sight from previous encounters.

On the night of October 31, 1933, a man fitting Verne's description was seen entering Vi's apartment, so everyone was called into place. Rogers and Notesteen wedged themselves into a tiny, sweltering cupboard which, when the door was open a crack, gave them a view to the back door of Vi's apartment. It was the second day of surveillance, November 1, when the agents were tipped by a call from Vi to Bobbie asking her to bring the car around. Everyone was on alert when Rogers heard the door open and saw a man step out. She recognized Verne immediately, and said so, but Notesteen was not sure.

Verne gets away one last time

"That's Miller!" Rogers whispered to Notesteen a second time—and, it seems, this time loud enough that Verne heard her. He threw open the stairwell door and slammed it after him as he ran down the one flight of stairs to the lobby. All the agents in the adjoining apartment raced out in a panic after him. Verne passed the group of agents in the lobby by blending in with other residents present. Two agents in the street watched Verne walk quickly out the doors and cross the street to a waiting car. They had seen Bobbie pull up in the car minutes earlier, but assumed she was waiting for her boyfriend, the building manager. An agent on the second floor was supposed to wave a white handkerchief out the window to warn them Verne was on his way, but in all the pandemonium the signal was forgotten.

Just as the agents rushed out and onto the street,

Verne jumped into Bobbie's car, but managed to fire two shots. Both missed. As the car sped away, one agent ran to the middle of the street and fired his weapon at the disappearing vehicle to no avail. The next day, newspapers reported that this was the first time law enforcement officers had ever fired a machine gun in Chicago streets.

Hoover was embarrassed and outraged at yet another blunder by his men. The newspapers were quick to point out that the federal agents had not asked for the assistance of the Chicago police, implying that events might have ended differently if they had sought their help. But Vi was taken into custody immediately and Bobbie, slightly wounded in the escape, surrendered two days later.

The pressure was on to find Verne Miller. His friends had all turned their backs on him—and one notable friend in particular. Buchalter was less than thrilled about the scrutiny his businesses were taking thanks to recent events. Furthermore, a valued lieutenant in Buchalter's organization, Al Silvers, had just been found by federal agents to be tied to Verne. On November 20, 1933, Silvers' body was found in a Connecticut ditch. He had been beaten about the head and then received two stab wounds to the heart.

Bureau agents paid a visit to Buchalter on November 28. He claimed to have nothing to offer on the death of Silvers, but also acknowledged that no one in the underworld would have anything to do with Verne anymore. When asked outright by the agents if he thought Verne might be murdered in the next 30 days, Buchalter replied simply, "Let me look into that."

The next day, Vi and Bobbie both appeared in court, having pleaded guilty to aiding and abetting a fugitive. They received sentences of a year and a day. Later that afternoon, a nude and brutally beaten body was found on the outskirts of Detroit. The story of Verne Miller had come to an end.

Bureau agents rushed to get the news to Bobbie and Vi, hoping to glean some valuable information from them. Bobbie was approached first. When she heard that Verne had been "knocked off up in Detroit," her "face paled and her lower lip trembled but she did not weep," the *Chicago Daily Tribune* reported.

Her cell was directly below Vi's and although there was no direct communication between them, she must have somehow told her friend the news, for when the agents arrived at Vi's cell, she was already sobbing.

"Then in a fit of hysteria she raged at the caller and demanded to be left alone. At the sound of her shrieks, Bobbie Moore also gave way to tears."

Neither woman revealed anything, but the feds

were not finished with Vi. She was released early on parole, suddenly and without warning. This did not leave her time to make arrangements to have someone meet her. Federal agents had their own plans. They picked her up and took her to an apartment, where she was held hostage and interrogated for 12 days. But she had been with Verne far too long to fall for any amateur tricks meant to make her talk. She was then taken to Chicago and interrogated by agent Sam McKee. It took him less than 12 hours to "break" her—he did so by holding lit cigarettes against her arms. She dictated and signed a statement regarding her knowledge of the Kansas City Massacre. Finally she was allowed to go home to her parents' farm. The burns she suffered at McKee's hands were deep and had become infected. It took Vi the next seven months to recover.

Emotionally, however, Vi never did get better. In 1935 she began working in a hotel and drinking heavily, losing contact most of the time with her family. In 1941, she married the hotel owner, Bob Kennedy, also a drinker and a violent man. Three years later, Vi died in hospital at the age of 38 from what was listed officially as tuberculosis.

When her physician brother examined his sister's body at the funeral home, he noticed it was covered with bruises in keeping with someone who had recently received a beating. The family did not pursue it. Their once outgoing, thrill-seeking girl had clearly given up the fight when she lost Verne, and they resigned themselves to leaving it that way.

Chapter Five

BONNIE PARKER AND CLYDE BARROW

Bonnie Parker sat with her cousin Mary in a car outside 625 Turner Avenue in East Waco, Texas, getting ready to break into the house. Bonnie was far from an angel, but it was the first time the young woman had ever done anything like this. Five days earlier, on March 3, 1930, she had driven to Waco with Clyde Barrow's mother to visit him in prison. She had missed him desperately and for the next five days the two young lovers met frequently. The tone of the visits changed, however, on March 8 when Bonnie told Clyde she could not stand to see him "cooped up like this."

"Maybe you won't have to much longer," Clyde's new cellmate, William Turner, told Bonnie.

"What are you talking about?" she asked.

Clyde stayed quiet as Turner outlined a plan to Bonnie. His parents, who lived in Waco, were going to be out late that night. Bonnie could slip into the house, find Turner's hidden gun, and bring it back to

Clyde Barrow poses with his lover, Bonnie Parker, in front of their car.

Clyde. This would allow the two men to break out of the prison.

"Is this what you want, Clyde?" Bonnie asked.

"It's a way to get me out of here and us together sooner," he replied.

That was all Bonnie needed to hear. Turner gave her the address and a sketch of the interior of the house.

Mary was appalled and frightened when she heard from her cousin what they were going to do, but she agreed to help. Bonnie located the key over the door-sill, unlocked the door and stepped inside. It took the two women some time, but finally they succeeded in finding the gun. Darkness was setting in as they raced back toward the jail, Bonnie all the while trying to figure out how she was going to smuggle the gun to Clyde. She ended up hiding it inside her dress and had little trouble passing it to her lover before the visit was over.

Lying in bed that night, Bonnie must have realized the gravity of what she had just done—breaking into a house for a gun and then smuggling it into prison where it was going to be used in a jail break. Bonnie Parker had now officially stepped over to the other side of the law.

Born October 1, 1910, in Rowena, Texas, to Charles and Emma Parker, Bonnie was the middle of three children. Her father was a brick mason who died when Bonnie was only four, resulting in the family's relocation to the Dallas suburb of Cement City to live with Emma's parents. Bonnie was a mischievous child, but a good student who excelled in spelling and creative writing. She stopped growing when she reached just 4 feet 10 inches in height and never weighed more than 90 pounds, but she was an attractive girl and the boys began to flock around. She quickly developed an eye for the "bad boys"—and her first was Roy Thornton. He was less than a year older than Bonnie's fifteen years when they met and started dating in high school, but he had already served time in a reform school. They married on September 26, 1926, five days before Bonnie's 16th birthday, and soon moved in with her mother. Celebrating their love, Bonnie had a tattoo of double hearts containing their names engraved on her thigh, above her right knee.

During the next year, Thornton twice left Bonnie alone for weeks at a time and then for a third time in December. She mourned and filled her time with friends and the movies. But after the last time she told herself that even if he returned she would not take him back. True to her word, when Thornton finally showed up early in 1929, she sent him packing for good. Shortly afterward, he joined a gang, got himself arrested for robbery, and was sent to jail. He was killed during a jail break in 1937.

By 1929, Bonnie was dating other men and working as a waitress in a number of cafés. It was in one of those that Ted Hinton, a local policeman, first came in contact with her. In his 1979 book *Ambush* (co-authored with Larry Grove), Hinton described Bonnie as "a very pretty young woman with taffy-colored hair that glistened red in the sun and with a complexion that was fair and tended to freckle . . . Bonnie could turn heads." In a conversation they had back then, she told him she wanted to be a poet or an entertainer.

Bonnie and Clyde meet

When the US stock market crashed in 1929 and the country struggled with an economic depression, Bonnie soon found herself out of work. One day in January 1930, she was helping out a neighbor who had recently broken her arm. Bonnie was in the kitchen making hot chocolate when in walked destiny —a young man who had just dropped by to see how a former girlfriend was doing.

Clyde Chestnut Barrow was just shy of 5 foot 7 inches tall and about 130 pounds. He had thick brown hair, slicked back, and dark brown eyes.

Born near Teleco, Texas, March 24, 1909, Clyde was one of the seven children of Henry and Cumie Barrow. The family moved often, following the crop harvests, but eventually settled in a squalid campground in West Dallas. Clyde did attend high school for a time and developed an interest in music, especially the guitar and saxophone. When his father managed to scrape together enough money to buy a small frame house, Clyde helped him convert the front part of the structure into a gas station and garage. The young man's connection to his family was strong then, as it remained throughout his life, but it wasn't enough to keep him on the straight and narrow. Before long, Clyde began to carry out minor robberies with a group of friends.

And that's where things stood when he wandered into the kitchen that fateful day at his old girlfriend's house—and found Bonnie. He introduced himself and from that moment on the two were inseparable, except when the law intervened.

In February, less than a month after they met, Clyde showed up at Bonnie's home and told her he had to leave town because the police were looking for him. Bonnie and her mother persuaded him to stay until morning, but before it came the police showed up to arrest him. While being held in Denton,

Texas (on charges that were later dropped), Clyde received a letter from Bonnie.

"When you get out I want you to go to work, and for God's sake don't ever get into anymore trouble," she wrote.

Clyde was released, but the authorities in Waco wanted him transferred there for a hearing related to several local burglaries. Bonnie begged her mother for the money to go to Waco and visit Clyde. Her mother refused, but did finally allow her daughter to drive there with Clyde's mother and stay with her cousin Mary.

A week later, after smuggling the gun to Clyde in jail, Bonnie returned home and waited to hear from him. The escape went off as planned and he sent Bonnie a wire, pledging his love and promising to be in touch. He quickly fell back to robbery and it wasn't long before he was arrested again in Ohio and this time sent to the Texas State Penitentiary for 14 years. Bonnie was listed as his wife when he entered the prison, which meant the two could correspond. Clyde was housed in the Eastham Prison Farm – which he forever after referred to as the "hell hole." In his 2000 book *The Family Story of Bonnie and Clyde*, author Phillip Steele wrote that, according to Clyde's mother, her son had been raped by a muscle-bound inmate while at the Eastham prison. Such an experience likely goes a long way in explaining Clyde's determination never to return to prison, whatever the cost.

As time went by, the correspondence between Clyde and Bonnie waned. Bonnie found the letters simply fueled the pain of not having him around. All this time, Clyde's mother had been working hard to get her son's sentence reduced to two years. Not knowing she was just about to succeed, Clyde decided to speed things along by having a fellow prisoner "accidentally" chop off two of his toes. He had heard Bonnie had started dating again and was afraid she would not wait for him. Clyde was promptly moved to hospital to recover, and it was from there that he was released on February 8, 1932. Instantly the two lovers were together again.

The two-year separation behind them, Bonnie and Clyde renewed their commitment to each other, and made a plan to be together in Houston. Bonnie, now 22, told her mother that she'd found a job there and was moving. What Mrs. Parker didn't know was that Bonnie would be living with Clyde. He, meanwhile, was busy setting up a gang and the first two recruits were Raymond Hamilton and Ralph Fults. Bonnie joined them on April 18, 1932, for both the first robbery in Kaufman, Texas—at which they failed—and the subsequent breaking and entering of a hardware store. They were looking for guns and ammunition. A sharp night watchman tripped the alarm, and the group was on the run for the first time. Hamilton and Fults escaped and Clyde put Bonnie in a culvert by the side of the road, promising to come back for her after he found a car. He never returned. A day later, tired and hungry, Bonnie crawled out to the highway and began hitch-hiking. Unfortunately, the person who picked her up turned out to be a member of the posse looking for the would-be burglars. She ended up sitting in jail for weeks waiting for the Grand Jury to meet. Clyde may have been missing her, but he managed to keep himself busy. He and Raymond Hamilton had now joined forces with Frank Chase and continued to commit burglaries.

The killing begins

It was during a store robbery that the killing began, albeit accidentally. Hamilton's finger slipped on a gun he was holding and it fired, killing the owner, John Bucher, instantly. When Mrs. Bucher later identified both Clyde and Hamilton from photos, there was no surrendering or turning back then.

"I'm just going on 'til they get me," Clyde told his sister Nell. "Then I'm out like Lottie's eye."

When Bonnie was finally released in June, she

assured her mother she was finished with Clyde forever. It was a promise she couldn't keep. In short order, she left for Wichita Falls, Texas, where she got a job as a waitress and moved back in with Clyde while he and Hamilton committed a crime wave throughout the northern part of the state.

In early August 1932, after hiding out in an abandoned farmhouse, Clyde dropped Bonnie off at her mother's. Like Clyde, Bonnie was close to her family, and especially her mother. The frantic and dangerous lives they led never kept them from risking everything to venture home for visits with both their families.

While Bonnie was at home, Clyde, Hamilton, and Everett Milligan crossed the border into Oklahoma, looking for likely businesses to rob. In Stringtown, they came upon an open-air dance floor. Hamilton, who had been drinking moonshine steadily, wanted them to stop and go dancing for a bit. Clyde reluctantly agreed. Unbeknownst to the men, Stringtown was a place where prohibition was being strictly enforced by the local police. When a couple of police officers spotted Hamilton drinking, they approached the car where he and Clyde were sitting while Milligan was still on the dance floor.

"Consider yourselves under arrest, gentlemen," Sheriff C.G. Maxwell announced.

Had it been only the threat of arrest for drinking, Clyde and Hamilton might have reacted differently. But, being who they were and knowing where an arrest would lead, they instantly pulled out their pistols and started blasting. The sheriff was seriously injured and his deputy killed instantly. Milligan, hearing the shots, blended into the dance crowd and disappeared, only to be captured the next day. Clyde and Hamilton, however, escaped in their car, racing along country roads back to the abandoned farmhouse in Texas.

Clyde became known for his ability to pull off the fast getaway. W.D. Jones, who ran with Bonnie and Clyde for more than eight months, wrote in a 1968 article in *Playboy Magazine*, "Ted Hinton and Bob Alcorn, the Dallas lawmen I come to know a year later, told me Clyde was about the best driver in the world. They said them Fords and Clyde's driving was what kept him and Bonnie free them two years. Hell. I knowed that. I rode with them."

Still visiting her family, Bonnie was just in the midst of telling her mother her intention to move to Wichita Falls to start a new life when Hamilton drove up to the house. When she went out to talk to him, he told her that Clyde was waiting for her at the hideout. It was the moment of truth for Bonnie Parker, and she did not hesitate. She went back into the house and told her mother that her ride to Wichita Falls had shown up. She also told her mother that she loved her. And then Bonnie walked toward her life with Clyde and never again considered giving it up.

The legend of Bonnie and Clyde

The group needed somewhere to lie low for a few days and chose the farm of Bonnie's aunt near Carlsbad, New Mexico. The aunt did not know who the men were, but she was suspicious of them and contacted the police. On August 14, 1932, Sheriff W. L. McDonald and Deputy-Sheriff Joe Johns approached the farm, primarily to look at the vehicle driven by the trio. They suspected it was stolen, but they had no idea who they were dealing with. While they were examining the vehicle, Bonnie, Clyde, and Hamilton all came out of the farm quickly with one of the men firing a shot at Johns, knocking his hat off.

They kidnapped Johns at gunpoint, stripped the ignition of the officer's car, and drove off, shooting at McDonald as they left. Posses were formed, wires sent out, and even army planes were used to try to find them, but as the hours passed with no sign of the vehicle, officials became convinced that Johns was dead. In fact, the outlaws took the officer for a wild journey of several hundred miles before releasing him. During the ride Johns said he talked them out of returning to kill Bonnie's aunt for phoning the sheriff's office. One of the abductors, he said, was called Raymond Hamilton. When he asked the names of the other two, they proudly told him "Bonnie and Clyde." This is how they were now forever known to law enforcement, and to the world.

Throughout the fall of 1932, the Barrow gang had various accomplices come and go as they continued to rob, and occasionally kill, all over Texas. Unlike the heists pulled off by members of the Dillinger Gang and Verne Miller, the robberies committed by Clyde and his partners netted very small amounts of money—just enough to give them something to live on for a few weeks before they did another one. Clyde didn't seem to aspire to greater wealth or the fame of pulling off bigger holdups. Although widely written about in newspapers at the time, the duo might have been just a footnote in history had the 1967 movie *Bonnie and Clyde* not been made. It vaulted them into almost mythic status and spawned dozens of books about their escapades.

Clyde did not allow Bonnie to take part in the actual robberies, but she often cased locations for them. Hamilton left the gang and then, during a Christmas reunion with their families, Clyde acknowledged he was worn out. He decided they needed someone he could trust to join them so that he and Bonnie wouldn't always need to be on guard. William Daniel (W.D.) Jones filled the bill. Only sixteen years old, he had grown up in the Barrow neighborhood and Clyde knew him well.

"He wanted me to go with them so I could keep watch while they got some rest," Jones related in the 1968 *Playboy* article. "I went. I know now it was a fool thing to do, but then it seemed sort of big to be out with two famous outlaws."

Jones quickly regretted his decision, for within a couple of days he was involved in the killing of a man who was trying to thwart Clyde's theft of his car.

"Boy, you can't go home," Clyde told Jones afterward. "You got murder on you, just like me."

According to Jones, Clyde never wanted to kill, but he did so "without hesitation when he had to, because he wanted to stay free . . . and Bonnie just wanted to be with Clyde."

The presence of Jones did give the couple time to rest and enjoy themselves from time to time. Bonnie and Clyde loved to have their photo taken and always carried a Kodak box camera with them.

Many of the famous photos of the pair were taken during the time Jones spent with them, including the one of Bonnie with a gun in her hand, foot up on the bumper of a car, and a cigar in her mouth. It was a set-up.

"I guess I got that started when I gave her my cigar to hold when I was making her picture," Jones said. Bonnie hated that photo, especially when it showed up in all the newspapers. In spite of loving her growing celebrity, she was irritated that people thought she smoked cigars, something she felt was unwomanly. "Tell them I don't smoke cigars," Bonnie later instructed a hostage when asked what she wanted relayed to the newspapers.

Clyde always kept a gun within arm's length, "even in bed, or out of bed on the floor in the night," said Jones, adding another interesting fact, "when he thought we was all asleep and couldn't see him kneeling there. I seen it more than once. He prayed. I reckon he was praying for his soul. Maybe it was for more life."

Jones always maintained he'd never once seen Bonnie shoot a firearm. "During the five big gun battles I was with them, she never fired a gun," he wrote. "But I'll say she was a hell of a loader."

Jones was surprised 30 years later to start hearing rumors about Clyde's sexuality. "I've heard stories since that Clyde was homosexual, or, as they say in the pen, a 'punk,' but they ain't true," he said, adding that he knew many of the convicts who had been with Clyde in prison and none of them ever mentioned it. "Maybe it was Clyde's quiet, polite manner and his slight build that fooled folks . . . I was with him and Bonnie. I know. It just ain't true."

Brother Buck joins the gang

Jones was still with Bonnie and Clyde in March 1933 when Clyde's older brother, Marvin "Buck" Barrow, was paroled. His wife, Blanche, was hoping that he would now put his criminal past behind him, but Buck wanted to talk things over with Clyde first. A reunion took place in April in Joplin, Missouri. Bonnie, Clyde, and Jones were renting a small apartment, chosen because it had a garage beneath it. In spite of her concerns (or maybe because of them), Blanche accompanied her husband on the one-month trip. The visit went well at the beginning as they laid low and did not draw attention to themselves. However, as their funds dwindled, Clyde began to scout locations to rob. About the same time, some neighbors were starting to wonder about who was living in the apartment and what they were doing. Someone contacted the police.

On April 13, Clyde and Jones left to go on another robbery reconnaissance mission. For some reason, they returned home early, at around 4:00 p.m. After backing into the garage, Clyde was lowering the garage door when a police car arrived in front of the building. Seeing the garage door still slightly open, the driver pulled straight up to it. As Constable John Harryman leapt from the car and ran to lift the door, a sawed-off shotgun appeared beneath it and fired, killing him instantly. Another blast from a Barrow gun (whose is unknown) nearly severed the hand of Detective Harry McGinnis as he jumped from the car. He also took shotgun blasts to his stomach and died later in hospital. The third officer fired at the garage from behind his vehicle. When the shooting started, Blanche had become hysterical and, in all the confusion, ran from the building and down the street. The rest all piled into the car and Clyde smashed the V-8 Ford through the partially open garage door and careened down the street after Blanche, stopping only long enough for Buck to grab his distraught wife and bundle her into the vehicle with them.

Although they escaped once again, the gang this time left behind enough evidence to identify all of them. Also found were two rolls of undeveloped film. This was the beginning of Bonnie and Clyde's true celebrity, as the newspapers clamored to fill their pages with photos of the two outlaws in various poses, showing off their love for guns and each other.

The heat on them was increasing, but both couples were missing their families—so much so that Blanche was sent ahead to arrange a reunion. The families all knew their phones were tapped, so they had a signal for relaying information to each other about any impending visit. Mrs. Barrow would phone the others, including Mrs. Parker, and say, "I'm cooking pinto beans for supper. Why don't you come over?"

When she saw her daughter this time, Bonnie's mother begged her to leave Clyde and surrender to the law.

"We both know Clyde will be killed," Bonnie replied. "When he dies, Mama, I will not have a reason to keep living, so I want to go with him."

Buck and Blanche were still visiting Blanche's family, but Jones was with Bonnie and Clyde on June 10, 1933, as they sped along the highway toward Wellington, Texas, at their usual 70 miles an hour. Without any road signs to warn them, they suddenly found themselves hurtling into the air where a bridge had just been removed. The car flew over the edge of the ravine and rolled several times before landing on its top. Clyde got himself free and quickly pulled Jones out. Then they pulled all the guns and ammunition away from the car. By this time, Bonnie, who was pinned under the wreckage, was screaming to Clyde for help. The two slight men could not budge it. Gasoline began to drip and in a second a spark ignited it. As the gasoline trickled onto Bonnie's legs, the flames followed. She howled in pain, her nylon stocking melting to her skin. Still Clyde and Jones could not free her. By sheer luck, two farmers who had seen the accident rushed down to help. Together the four men were able to pull Bonnie from the fire and mangled metal and throw sand and dirt on her to smother the flames.

"She'd been burned so bad none of us thought she was gonna live," Jones said. "The hide on her right leg was gone, from her hip down to her ankle. I could see the bone at places."

Taken to a farmhouse, Bonnie got her wounds washed and bandaged. However, one of the farmers had become uneasy at the sight of all the weapons and phoned the local sheriff. When two lawmen showed up at the farm, they were immediately taken hostage by Clyde. One of them was ordered into the back seat of his own car with Bonnie across his lap. With the other in the front seat with Jones, Clyde headed toward a rendezvous with Buck and Blanche. Three hours later at the rendezvous, Clyde decided to spare the lawmen's lives, "thinking how gentle they had been with Bonnie," Jones said.

In spite of the alert put out by the released lawmen, Clyde once again slipped the trap and the gang headed to Fort Smith, Arkansas, where they rented a couple of cabins at the Dennis Tourist Courts. With Bonnie's burns being so severe, Clyde drove to Dallas and brought back her sister Billie to care for her. Surprisingly, they also received help from the Dennis family, who gave them money, food, and medical supplies even though they knew they had the Barrow gang on their premises.

After a couple of weeks, and with funds getting low, Clyde sent Buck and Jones off to do a job on their own. During their escape from that robbery, the two killed yet another lawman. It was time to go. The group passed through Oklahoma and into Texas again, dropping Billie off at a railroad depot to catch a train home. Clyde felt it was too dangerous for her to remain with them.

On July 18, 1933, the tired group pulled into the Red Crown Tourist Camp near Platte City, Missouri. They rented two cabins with a garage in between, as usual backing their vehicle in for an easy getaway. They had no idea that the desk clerk had recognized them and alerted police. At 1:00 a.m. on July 19, the cabins were surrounded by a posse. This time it really looked like the end was at hand.

"This is the police! Open up!" hollered Sheriff Holt Coffey as he banged on the door of the cabin in which Buck and Blanche were sleeping.

"You'll have to wait until I'm dressed!" Blanche called back from inside.

What Coffey and his men didn't know was that the Barrow gang had recently knocked over a National Guard supply depot. The firearms they had on hand were military-issue Browning assault rifles—very powerful weapons. Before he knew what happened, Coffey was hit from all sides by a blast of gunfire, suffering a major wound to his neck. He gamely fought back. The rifles were so powerful, however, their fire even penetrated the armored car blocking the garage, wounding the occupants and forcing them to move the vehicle out of the line of fire. This was the only opening Clyde needed and he quickly piled all their weapons into the car.

Buck Barrow then sprang from his cabin and began to spray bullets wildly around the parking lot. While many officers fled for cover, Coffey and several others fired back. One bullet struck Buck in the head and sent him reeling backward, his Browning still spitting bullets. Seeing Buck down, Blanche ran out of the cabin, clutching an assault rifle, too. Clyde, who had just carried Bonnie to the car, then ran to help his wounded brother into the vehicle. All five of them safely in the car, Clyde roared out of the garage with Jones on the right running board, showering the officers with his rifle. Return bullets from the officers smashed the car's windows and a glass shard struck Blanche in her left eye.

"I'm blind! I'm blind!" she shrieked as the car sped away.

Clyde found a country road and drove with the lights off for a while until they came to an open field. He spread newspapers on the grass and they laid Buck on the ground. Having recently stolen a car containing a doctor's kit, they at least had some means of treating the injured man. Clyde poured peroxide into the open wound and then tried to help Blanche with her bleeding eye. (In spite of four later surgeries, Blanche ended up losing the sight in the eye permanently.)

While scouting the area for escape routes, Clyde disposed of a bag of bloody bandages from the wounds. He knew it would be dangerous for them if it was found, so he set it on fire and left it. A few days later, a local farmer came upon the only partially burned rags and phoned police. Within 24 hours, a posse of 40 officers and 100 farmers moved into place around the outlaws, determined to capture them. Meanwhile, Clyde, who could see that Buck was dying, wanted to return him home and so, on the morning of July 24, he was making plans to leave for Texas.

Bonnie was the first one to see the posse.

"Clyde—it's the law!" she yelled.

Both Clyde and Jones opened fire on the incoming attackers to give Bonnie, Buck, and Blanche, crippled by their various injuries, time to crawl to the car. When they were finally in, Clyde and Jones leapt in too. As the car started to pull away, bullets ripped into Clyde's arm and he lost control of the car and crashed. They stumbled to a second car nearby, only to find it had been disabled by bullets. That left them only one more choice: to go for cover.

Buck was hit in the chest and back almost immediately and fell to the ground with Blanche clinging to him and screaming for help. Jones was also hit and then Clyde, dragging Buck into the bushes, got shot in the leg. Nevertheless, he told the others he would find a car and return for them. He left Jones to look after Bonnie. Just beyond the field was a river. Clyde limped toward it, hoping to cross it and find a car to steal. While Jones helped Bonnie head slowly for the river as well, members of the posse moved in and took Buck and Blanche into custody. Then, when Jones and Bonnie heard a barrage of gunfire from up ahead, Bonnie burst into sobs of despair thinking Clyde was dead for sure. Even Jones started to cry—but the two of them stopped abruptly when, seconds later, Clyde appeared and came again to their aid.

With bullets flying everywhere, the trio reached the river. By some miracle, they escaped and made their way to a farmhouse. Once more, Clyde stole a vehicle and drove the injured trio to safety. After he washed Jones's wounds so that he could drive, Clyde passed out from loss of blood. They found a wooded area near Colorado City and rested for several days until they were strong enough for Clyde to resume the driving. Relieved of that responsibility, Jones took the opportunity to disappear into the night. He had decided that he wanted to live.

Death on the back roads

With Jones gone, Bonnie and Clyde were now alone. Buck, they soon learned, had died in hospital on July 29 and Blanche was in prison. The outlaw couple lay low over the next four months, committing few crimes (although they were falsely credited with many during that period). In late November 1933, an attempted reunion with their families ended with the two fugitives racing away down a back road as pursuing officials fired at them—more wounds but another escape.

As 1934 began, word reached Bonnie and Clyde that their old cohort Raymond Hamilton wanted their help in breaking out of Eastham Prison Farm. They were happy to oblige. On January 14, Clyde was at the wheel of the car that drove Hamilton and several other prisoners away to freedom. One of those other escapees was Henry Methvin. During the escape a guard was killed.

The prison break was the last straw for the Texas Department of Corrections, which repeatedly looked incompetent. Lee Simmons, Director of Texas Prisons, finally received permission from the Governor of Texas to form a special task force to stop Bonnie and Clyde—by whatever means. And for Simmons there was only one man he wanted to head the force: Texas Ranger Frank Hamer. Hamer had been involved in 50 shootouts in a career spanning three decades, and he had 23 facial scars to prove it. Five other lawmen from three different agencies joined him.

Soon afterward, Bonnie and Clyde joined with

Hamilton and Methvin to rob a bank. They were successful, but as they were driving away, Clyde caught sight in the rear view mirror of Hamilton stuffing some money into his shirt before the loot had been divided up. He dropped Hamilton off and vowed never to work with him again (Hamilton was arrested a year later and executed in 1935).

Then, on April 1, two young police officers approached the vehicle that Bonnie, Clyde, and Methvin were sitting in. Methvin had not been with Clyde long and didn't know about his penchant for kidnapping lawmen. He therefore misunderstood Clyde's directive "Let's take them" and immediately opened fire. Both officers died. Only four days later, a similar incident took place, with Clyde and Methvin killing an officer and wounding and then taking hostage a second one. With their car stuck in the mud, they flagged down another car and stole it. A day later, near Fort Scott, Kansas, they let the relieved officer go.

Early in May 1934, Bonnie and Clyde arranged to meet with their families once again, accompanied by Methvin. It was a bittersweet visit, filled with talk of death.

"When they kill us, don't let them take me to an undertaking parlor, will you?" Bonnie entreated her mother. "Bring me home." She also begged her mother not to say anything "ugly" about Clyde after their deaths.

One of Bonnie's favorite pastimes was writing poetry and before she left she gave her mother a poem she had written titled *The Story of Bonnie and Clyde*, part of which read:

> *Someday they'll go down together*
> *And they'll bury them side by side*
> *To few it'll be grief, to the law a relief*
> *But it's death for Bonnie and Clyde.*

As the car pulled away, Bonnie rolled down the window and waved at her family.

"We'll be back in two weeks, I promise," she said.

Hamer had assembled a group of six men to form his posse, one of whom was Ted Hinton—the same police officer who, in 1929, had admired the diminutive beauty serving him in a café. Methvin's father, Ivy Methvin, lived in Rushton, Louisiana, and Hamer had received word that the trio were on their way there to visit him.

It may be that hearing all the talk of death at Bonnie and Clyde's family reunion just a few weeks before had made Henry Methvin decide that he wanted a different future from the grimly inevitable one into which his two partners were riding—or maybe his father decided it for him. History will never know. The three had been in the Rushton area for a few days and on May 21 had attended a Methvin family party, where Ivy had encouraged his son to leave Bonnie and Clyde. The next morning, Henry made an excuse to go into town and simply disappeared. It was a timely departure.

On the evening of May 22, 1934, a few miles south of Gibsland, Louisiana, Ivy Methvin was stopped by the lawmen as he drove in his Model A Ford truck. They ordered him out, kidnapped him, and took him into the woods. There they handcuffed him to a tree so that he would not interfere in the events that followed. He would remain there throughout the night, not knowing whether or not his son was still with Bonnie and Clyde.

Many reports over the years have claimed that Ivy Methvin made a deal with Hamer to set up Bonnie and Clyde in order to save his son. In fact, the only deal Methvin Senior made was after what was about to unfold, when he later agreed to stay silent about his own kidnapping and what he'd witnessed if his son was pardoned. This version of events is substantiated by Ted Hinton's account in his book *Ambush*. The six men in Hamer's posse that day had sworn to hide the truth about what they were about to do until only one of them was left—and that ended up being Hinton, who died in 1977. A number of other versions of the final act state that Methvin had a more active role and may have even flagged the posse's car down.

Back at the road, the posse removed one of the Ford's wheels so that the truck looked disabled. Then the men concealed themselves in the bushes on either side of the road and settled down to wait. The hours passed and the mosquitoes bit and night turned into dawn. The group was close to giving up when, at 9:10 a.m., they finally heard a car in the distance. It was May 23.

Bonnie and Clyde's bullet-ridden car, the last in a long line of Fords that they used.

Bonnie was eating a sandwich and reading a detective magazine as Clyde raced along the dusty road. Their car was stocked with weapons of all kinds, and Clyde's saxophone and sheet music lay on the back seat. When he saw Methvin's disabled truck in the road, Clyde wondered if the old man needed help and began to slow down. Just then Bonnie looked up from her magazine and saw movement in the bushes. Hamer's "Shoot!", Bonnie's "long and painful" scream, explosions of gunfire, and the sound of 167 bullets ripping through the car all erupted at once, filling the quiet countryside with a deafening noise. Then there was silence.

"I scramble over the hood of the car and throw open the door on Bonnie's side," Hinton wrote. "The impression will linger with me from this instant . . . I see her falling out of the opened door, a beautiful and petite young girl . . . and I smell a light perfume against the burned-cordite smell of gunpowder."

Hinton's description of events later became somewhat suspect as some people said he became delusional later in life. What is not suspect was what happened in the aftermath of the shooting. Word of the ambush spread quickly and a crowd began to gather around the car with the bodies inside. The two officers left to guard the remains of Bonnie and Clyde were unable to control the crowd.

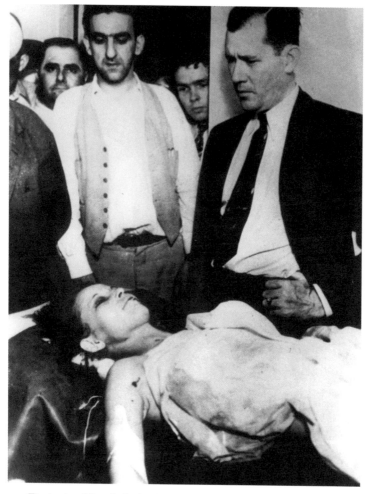

The body of Bonnie Parker lying in the morgue, surrounded by law enforcement officers.

In *The Lives and Times of Bonnie and Clyde*, E.R. Milner wrote that when the coroner arrived he said that "nearly everyone had begun collecting souvenirs such as shell casings, slivers of glass from the shattered car windows, and bloody pieces of clothing from the garments of Bonnie and Clyde. One eager man had opened his pocket knife, and was reaching into the car to cut off Clyde's left ear."

It was not only members of the public who got into the act. Many of the items in the car were reportedly stolen by various law enforcement officials. A member of the Barrow family said that one of the officials kept a suitcase full of cash. This official later made a substantial land purchase. The line between gangster and law official was often a tenuous one.

Through the deal his father set up, Henry Methvin was pardoned of any crimes in Texas, but Oklahoma had not agreed to such a deal and he was tried and sentenced to die. This penalty was eventually reduced to a ten-year sentence. After his early release in 1942 he slipped into alcoholism and the life of a hobo. His death came in 1949 as he fell drunk on the railway tracks and was run over by a train. As with all the other stories around the legend of Bonnie and Clyde, there was another version of Methvin's death, one in which he was pushed in front of the train in payback for the ultimate betrayal of the couple. His father, who without a doubt played some role in the ambush, died in a hit and run accident in 1946. This too was shrouded in theories that it was no accident.

Chapter Six

WOMEN IN THE MOB: VIRGINIA HILL AND BUGSY SIEGEL

As the 1930s drew to a close, most of the gangsters who had been given extensive press coverage were dead. Their gun molls were dead or in prison for harboring them or had faded into the sunset. The women had been trapped by love and perhaps the excitement, but their lives could never have been called glamorous, in spite of how the press painted it. With the gangster era mostly defunct, the press turned their attention to the lives of the mobsters, who were more sophisticated, more organized, and very much richer than their gangster cousins had been. The mistresses who walked by their side did so for the glamour and the riches, and, as the gun molls before them, occasionally for the excitement.

Some of the women were not only mistresses but also players within the Mob themselves. Virginia Hill fell into this category even if she tried to convince officials otherwise. The Senate's Kefauver Committee, set up to examine organized crime in America and chaired by Tennessee Senator Estes Kefauver, was in full swing in 1951 and the proceedings were extensively televised. The American public watched day after day as a succession of mobsters were grilled by the committee members about their activities. However, it would be a woman who would take centre stage in March, when Virginia Hill—dubbed the "Mob Queen" by the press—faced them all down.

Her lover Bugsy Siegel had been dead for four years, but she had lost none of the feistiness that defined their relationship. In public portions of her testimony, she revealed more than most expected, but it was in her closed-door testimony that she did most to shock the senators. They constantly pushed her for an answer as to why so many powerful criminal men would just give her money. She tried to be evasive, but the committee members kept pressuring her. Finally, she could stand it no longer.

You really want to know why, she asked. Haughtily, one senator said he did. Her short explanation would have embarrassed even a longshoreman.

"Because I am the best goddamned c***s****r in America," she replied.

The committee went silent, and so ended that line of questioning.

Virginia Hill, who straddled the line between being a mobster's moll and being a mobster herself.

Virginia Hill was a saucy mixture of sophistication and crudeness. "She posed as a lady of refinement and dignity, but could be a vulgar alcoholic who shimmied barefoot in public bars and used language salty enough to make most truck drivers blush," Andy Edmonds wrote of her in *Bugsy's Baby*.

The girl who grew up fast—and loose

Virginia learned to be tough at a very young age. Born Onie Virginia Hill on August 26, 1916, in Lipscomb, Alabama, she was the seventh of ten children. Her father, a horse and mule trader, was a vicious drunk who beat his wife and kids. He was especially hard on Virginia, who was a small and passive child—until one day, when she was about seven years old, she hit him with an iron skillet sizzling with grease. He never touched her again. With that, Virginia gained a strong sense of herself, but her opinion of men remained poisoned for life.

In the mid-1920s, Virginia's mother finally took the children and left for Marietta, Georgia. By the time she reached her teens, Virginia had blossomed into a 5-foot 4-inch beauty with auburn hair and blue-grey eyes. She also had sexual experience far beyond her years, learning early on to use her body to get whatever she wanted from men. Marietta was soon not big enough to hold her, so Virginia set her sights on Chicago.

The Century of Progress Exposition was a world's fair held in Chicago in 1933. It was so successful that it carried over for 1934 as well. The theme of the fair was technological innovation, something Virginia cared little about—but to the 17-year-old it meant the potential for work. She was successful in that quest, and ended up doing a variety of jobs there, including being a dancer and waitress. It was in the latter capacity that Virginia got her first introduction to the underworld. Joe Epstein, an assistant in laundering Mob profits for Al Capone, was a regular at the café where she worked. He was a quiet, bookworm type who nevertheless loved to party. While he was both smitten and intrigued by Virginia, she was friendly but not at first particularly interested in him or the Mob friends he brought around.

Coincidentally, however, also through the café, Virginia had met and become friends with Capone's sister-in-law. One evening, the two women crashed a Mob party. Epstein was there and he and Virginia talked all night. He had been looking for a woman like her whom he could take under his wing and use for business purposes. His main line of work was gambling and he needed a money carrier who was not a member of the Mob and was above suspicion by the police. During the next year, Epstein groomed Virginia in more ways than one. He introduced her to gambling and money laundering, he bought her the best of clothes, and he taught her to be more "high class" so that she could fit in with the big rollers in the gambling world. It paid off for both of them and Virginia quickly became an integral part of the organization.

In 1936, Epstein sent Virginia to New York, where she moved with ease into the underworld circles there. On orders from Epstein, she began an affair with Joey Adonis, an up-and-coming mobster whom Epstein wanted to keep an eye on. A woman of initiative, Virginia also started to keep, without anyone's knowledge, a very detailed diary of Mob activities.

Virginia meets Bugsy Siegel

It was in New York the following year that Virginia first met Ben "Bugsy" Siegel. He swept her off her feet and, within a day, into bed. Siegel, born in New York's Lower East Side, was quickly moving up the Mob ladder. From the age of 14 on, he had his own gang. He bragged about having committed every crime in the book, and once admitted to personally killing at least 12 people. His violent temper had earned him his nickname: when he was angry, he seemed to lose his mind, or "go buggy." Siegel hated the nickname and people were ill-advised to use it in front of him.

Virginia's involvement with Siegel put an end to her relationship with Adonis, but then just as quickly Siegel abruptly dropped her too. Virginia may have been hurt, but she still had work to do for Epstein and others. She moved to California for a time, and made frequent trips to Mexico on business for the Mob. In the next three years she also acquired and discarded three husbands. However, all of this activity did not stop her from reconnecting with Bugsy Siegel in 1939. Siegel had been sent to the West Coast by the New York Mob to develop gambling rackets for the Syndicate (a Mafia-based network). In no time he had taken over the Screen Extras Guild and the Los Angeles Teamsters. With control of the Guild, he shook down Warner Brothers Studio for $10,000, threatening to withhold extras from any of the movies. It worked.

And now the Chicago Mob wanted Virginia to get close to Siegel again so they could find a way of moving in on his operations. It was an assignment Virginia took on happily.

Though married for many years, Siegel was a compulsive womanizer, and getting back together with Virginia didn't change that. Of course, she got around herself. Theirs became a tumultuous relationship, as passionate in love as in fighting. She called him "Baby Blue Eyes" and he called her his "Flamingo" —and both, apparently, hated the nicknames.

Siegel was also a compulsive gambler who kept borrowing money from Virginia, a habit that wore thin with her. They were both extremely jealous and physically abusive with each other, leaving bruises and cuts that sometimes took weeks to heal. Many of the fights were over his refusal to divorce his wife. Finally, in 1944, a fight occurred that nearly ended things permanently. As Virginia tried to leave his home, Siegel dragged her back into the house, kicking and slapping her hard. She screamed at him over the borrowed money and then attacked his masculinity, saying she saw other men because he was such a lousy lover. It was a lie, but Virginia knew it would enrage him. She was right. Siegel went crazy, beating her nearly unconscious and then raping her.

Shortly after this episode, Siegel decided he'd had enough of Los Angeles and would move to Nevada. In a gesture typical of their bizarre relationship, he even asked Virginia to join him. To pay him back for the beating and rape, she refused his invitation and traveled instead to New York and back into the arms of Joey Adonis and several other men. Nevertheless, Virginia was still under instructions to keep an eye on Siegel for the Mob, so when he got busy building a large casino and hotel in the Las Vegas desert, she went back to him. In truth, as she would later say in interviews, she was genuinely drawn to Siegel—the only man, she claimed, she had ever loved.

Death comes to Siegel in Los Angeles

Las Vegas was known for its legal prostitution and gambling. Siegel already owned four small gambling joints, but he had higher aspirations. As he shared all his plans in detail with Virginia, she wrote everything down in notes for the Chicago Mob, adding extra entries in her diaries for herself.

The casino and hotel project—the first of its kind and the beginning of the modern Las Vegas—was going way over budget and the shareholders, including Meyer Lansky and his New York Mob, weren't happy. They also believed that Siegel was skimming money off the top—which he was, with Virginia depositing this money in Europe. At Christmas 1945, however, the doors opened on the new Flamingo Hotel—named, of course, after Virginia. The rooms were not ready, which meant guests could not actually stay there yet. The whole enterprise at this point was a complete disaster, resulting in the hotel closing down right after the holidays. Still, Siegel persisted and reopened in March, this time to greater success. As summer approached, the operation was even showing a profit. For the powers that be in Chicago, however, there were other bones to pick with Siegel. Not only was he controlling the wire services in the west and not sharing the profits with the Mob, he was also putting out feelers about starting his own western organization. Now the Chicago Mob was getting very angry with him.

On June 8, 1947, Virginia—not long after being on the receiving end of another beating by Siegel —got a phone call telling her to be in Chicago in two days. If he asked, she was to tell Siegel she was flying to Paris to buy wine for the Flamingo. Virginia didn't question it. She was met in Chicago by Epstein and she stayed there until June 16, when she flew to Paris without once talking to Siegel.

Arriving in Los Angeles on June 19, Siegel went to Virginia's house, where he always stayed when he was in town. He was disappointed not to find her there. The next evening, he and Allen Smiley, a Chicago mobster staying at the house with him, went out for dinner. When they returned home, it was 10:30 p.m. and Smiley opened the front drapes in the living room as Siegel sat down on the sofa and began to read the *Los Angeles Times*.

Siegel became bored with the paper and was restless, so Smiley offered to fix him a drink to relax him. Siegel accepted and Smiley left the room to make it. Siegel settled down again to read the paper. At exactly 10:45 p.m., nine shots were fired rapidly through the living room window. Four found their mark and Siegel was dead.

Virginia apparently fainted when she heard the news.

However, she did not go to Siegel's funeral, which was attended by only seven people, and was later quoted as saying that she didn't care "what route the b****** took to get to hell."

The murder was never officially solved, but it seemed more than coincidental that a few minutes after the shooting, two mobsters with gambling backgrounds walked up to the microphone at the Flamingo Hotel and announced that "we" were taking over. Nobody had to ask who "we" were.

Life after Siegel

Virginia's life without Siegel was initially difficult. She began drinking more and tried taking her life several times. During one suicide attempt, Virginia was found unconscious with her head resting on a photograph of her and Siegel. She was also frightened of the possibility the Mob might kill her. Had she known how close she came to being beside Siegel on the sofa that night in Los Angeles, she would have been even more frightened. What she didn't realize was that Adonis had gone to bat for her—a decision he later lived to regret.

One reason Virginia feared for her life was that, following Siegel's death, the police started circulating the lie that he had left behind a diary. They even "leaked" a few of the details, about such things as the dealings of the Guzik-Ricca-Capone mob and

Bugsy Siegel's bullet-ridden corpse on a sofa in Virginia's apartment in Beverly Hills.

bribes and shakedowns of Chicago "gin mills." There was no diary, but the mere threat of it stirred things up in the Mob and put Virginia on edge. She feared that if she had a starring role in any Siegel diary, it might lead to the Chicago Mob finding out she was spying on them for New York mobsters. That would mean certain death.

Months later, however, when no one was arrested for the murder of Siegel and no diary surfaced, Virginia began to relax. Her life returned to normal, and she resumed being given money by Epstein.

In February 1950, Virginia met and soon married Sun Valley ski instructor Hans Hauser. Although he had come from Austria before World War II, Hauser was still not a United States citizen. His marriage brought Immigration and Naturalization Service scrutiny, and not long after Virginia got into another well-publicized fight with the press, Hauser lost his job. Because his visa required him to be employed at all times while living in the U.S., he was now under risk of deportation.

Virginia appealed to all her old friends, as did Hauser, to help him obtain American citizenship, but their requests were rebuffed. The "Mob Queen" was furious at what she saw as a betrayal—so furious that for the first time she mentioned her diary and its explosive contents, including the names of mobsters and high-placed public officials. She didn't stop there.

As Edmonds wrote in *Bugsy's Baby*, "Hill also told reporters that she had served as a messenger for the Mob, had carried large sums of money between New

York and Chicago, and had received cash in shipments of $1,000 and more while in Paris during the Siegel murder."

Virginia added that although she had had nothing to do with it, she did know who had killed Siegel.

Virginia attracts the Government's attention

All this public boasting and bravado did not result in Hauser receiving his citizenship, but it did bring Virginia to the attention of the Senate Kefauver Committee. Virginia's private testimony created such a stir among the committee members that the government decided the closed-door testimony would be sealed.

Then the public portion took place. More than 86 percent of all homes in New York were tuned into the hearings. Virginia shone in front of the cameras on March 16, 1951, four months after giving birth to a son. Wearing a black suit with a silver-blue mink stole and a large black hat, she stepped out of her taxi to exploding flashbulbs and microphones in her face. She exploded herself, lambasting reporters with a string of epithets unfit to print.

Inside the hearing room, she was far more composed as she spent an hour answering questions. She told committee members that she'd been exceptionally lucky at gambling and this accounted for a lot of her wealth.

"If she bets on a horse it wins," the *Chicago Daily Tribune* reported. "If she starts a night club, it prospers so fast that her financial advisor, Joseph Epstein of Chicago, makes her give it away before she begins having trouble with the income tax people."

She insisted that no gangsters ever gave her money. "The men who gave me things were not gangsters or racketeers," Virginia told the committee with a straight face. "We went out and had a lot of fun together, and they gave me a lot of presents . . . they bought me a house in Florida." She also denied being "the queen of the Mexican narcotic racket." She admitted only to knowing a number of musicians who used dope.

Virginia Hill giving testimony in front of the Senate Kefauver Committee into organized crime.

When she finished her testimony, Virginia was given a rousing round of applause by the spectators. Outside the hearing room, however, she dropped the gloves again, slapping a female reporter in the face and kicking over a photographer kneeling to take her photo.

"I hope the atom bomb falls on every one of you!" she shouted back at the reporters as she left the building.

Still the press gave her appearance in front of the committee top marks. "It's Virginia Hill by a Mile in N.Y. Derby, Bookies Say," the headline in the paper read the next day. They said she left her questioners "in a cloud of dust," alluding to her luck at the racetrack.

Virginia may have won a victory over the Kefauver Committee, but her testimony created new problems. All her old Mob friends quickly turned their backs on her and doors slammed shut in quick succession. But not the Internal Revenue Service's door. With all Virginia's talk of money and wealth, the IRS was now very interested in her financial holdings. She and Hauser were constantly harassed from all sides and finally a deportation ordered was issued for him. He was told to leave the United States by September 1, 1951. That summer, the Treasury Department also filed liens against Virginia's Cook

County property and her home in Spokane, Washington. This was done as security against the $160,000 they claimed she owed in back taxes for the years 1944 through 1947. Virginia was particularly upset when she showed up at her Spokane home to find it locked up and all her belongings seized.

In August 1951, with Hauser and their son safely in Chile, Virginia's personal property, Cadillac, and Spokane home were all auctioned off by the government. They had seized and sold all her possessions and finally, when they were going to take away her freedom, she fled the United States. The family traveled through Europe for a few years before settling in Austria. The Hausers lived the life of the rich, and Virginia made up numerous stories to explain their wealth. In truth, however, from 1952 on, she received annual payments from the Mob: $25,000 bundled up and sent to her through a courier— Joe Epstein.

To ensure Virginia would not return to the U.S. for fear of arrest, the government indicted her in 1954 for tax evasion. They even put out a wanted poster for her, painting her publicly as a whore and a cheat. When word of this reached Virginia, she responded by slipping faster into alcoholism and letting her paranoia about everyone run wild. Hauser bore the worst of her rage and opted to leave her alone for long periods of time.

By 1956, Virginia decided the only way to get her life back on track was to return to the U.S. and so she began negotiations to bring this about. She not only contacted the government, but also Joey Adonis who, although living outside of the country by then, still had tremendous pull in the Mafia. Virginia wanted him to use that influence to get corrupt officials to help her. She had only one piece of leverage left to pull it all off—her diary. Negotiations with the government over the next couple of years almost came to fruition, but they wanted more from Virginia than she was willing to give.

In addition to agreeing to a short prison term, she was to revoke her Austrian citizenship and reclaim her American one. As well, she was to give testimony against members of the Mafia, including Epstein. Virginia refused to agree to the last condition. Even she had her limits: she was clear she would not testify against Epstein. The talks continued until finally Virginia felt she was not being treated fairly. In a huff, she decided the deal-making was over.

This turn of events sent her into another alcohol and pill-fuelled tailspin, and on April 20, 1965, she was rushed to a hospital in Salzburg, Austria, suffering from an overdose. It was here that investigators from Interpol, the International Police Organization, learned about the $25,000 a year she had been receiving from the Mob. Virginia told them that the flow of funds from Chicago had been stopped and that she was depressed over being unable to return to the United States. The suicide attempt was not made public at the time.

As 1966 began, Virginia had only one card left to play: blackmail members of the Mob with the diary. She wired Epstein for money, but added a threat to the bottom of the telegram. Feeling that he had been the one steadfast friend she had, he was upset by the threat. He did send the money, but added a threat of his own. If she did not return to the United States and accept whatever punishment the government handed out, the money ended. Not satisfied, Virginia contacted Adonis, who was by then living in Naples. He ignored her first telegram, but the second one in February 1966 was harder to dismiss. Unless he started sending her money, Virginia said, the diary would go to the United States government. She promptly received $3,000 and, at her request, another $3,000 in March.

Against explicit instructions never to do so, Virginia then tracked down Adonis by phone at his villa and asked to see him. He refused.

"Listen, you son of a bitch," she told him. "I need twenty thousand more. If you [expletive] believe you can just walk away, you're wrong [expletive]."

The conversation ended with her saying she could go back to the United States and give the authorities the diary. According to author Andy Edmonds, Virginia left her Salzburg hotel March 22, 1966, and flew to Naples to see Adonis. They made up, had a drink, ate, and talked before retiring for the night. The next day, Adonis tried to get her to give up the diary, but she refused. She wanted $10,000 to help her buy a house for herself and her son (by then, she was separated from Hauser) and get back on her feet. He reportedly gave her the money and Virginia left, promising never to contact him again. A couple of his men escorted her back to the train for Salzburg.

Two days later, on March 24, Virginia Hill, 49, was found dead near a brook in Koppl, Austria. The local officials reported the death as a suicide. At first, they had no idea of Virginia's true identity.

The "queen of the gangsters' molls,' as *Time* magazine had called her in March 1951, was no more. The same day she died, on the other side of the world—well before the news of her death had reached the U.S.—Joe Epstein fingered the safety deposit box key he'd received just three days earlier. It had been delivered to him in Chicago, arriving in an envelope with no note. Nevertheless, he knew it came from Virginia. In the box he found Virginia's diary, wrapped in brown butcher paper and tied with string. On the outside in Virginia's handwriting were the words "Open in case of emergency . . . or my death. Virginia Hill."

Before Epstein died in 1976, he passed the diary on to a close friend and member of the Chicago underworld. Its exact whereabouts remains unknown.

Whether Virginia really did take her own life or was poisoned has never been proven one way or the other, although a member of the Mob told author Edmonds it was the latter. Whatever the truth, it seems clear that Virginia knew her days were numbered. And in the end, she opted to protect the Mob by sending the diary to Epstein.

A Virginia Hill wannabe

Arlyne Weiss was a fourteen-year-old New Yorker when Virginia Hill appeared before the Kefauver Committee in 1951. Her father had made his money in the rackets and Arlyne already aspired to be in the Mob too. However, not until she saw a photo of Virginia Hill in the paper did her vision take shape. She read about Virginia's life and decided that "here was a broad that really made it good." There and then, Arlyne decided to become a Mob girl exactly like Virginia. She even fashioned herself to look like her idol and set out to be a moll.

What she didn't know then is how her ambitious yearnings would lead her into the story of another woman, Janice Drake, who also found the lure of mobsters too great to refuse.

Janice was born in the mid-1920s in New Jersey. A natural beauty who was a drum majorette in high school, she went on to become Miss New Jersey (1944) and then winner of a contest for having the "most beautiful legs in the United States." In 1945 she married comedian Alan Drake (who later appeared several times on *The Tonight Show* with Johnny Carson and in television episodes of *Get Smart* and *Sanford and Son*.) Neither her marriage, nor the birth of a son, stopped her from becoming well connected to mobsters.

It's not clear whether her associations with the underworld began through Drake or his associations there began with her. What is known is that they were both friends of mobster Anthony Carfano, or Little Augie Pisano as he was better known. Pisano had been an East Coast lieutenant of Al Capone and partners in many underworld ventures with Frank Costello and Charles "Lucky" Luciano. He had been arrested, indicted, taken into protective custody and questioned, but he had never been convicted of anything. And his show business connections had definitely helped Drake's career.

Janice Drake, sometime friend of mobsters, ended up as collateral damage in the assassination of New York gangster Anthony Carfano.

Drake was often on the West Coast working. Janice used his absences – and the license of their "open" marriage—to get out on the town. She loved to be part of the nightclub scene and was a popular Mob groupie. Her connections to the underworld brought her to the attention of the police on two occasions. In February 1952 she was taken in for questioning following the murder of mobster Nat Nelson because she had been seen with him in several Greenwich Village clubs the night before his murder. At the time, one of the many women Nelson had been seeing was the young mob wannabe Arlyne Weiss. She, in fact, discovered his body and knew his killer.

Five years later, Janice was taken in for questioning again, this time for a much more high-profile murder —that of mobster Albert Anastasia, someone with whom she had recently been out on the town. She was released and carried on as usual.

Janice called Pisano, almost twice her age, "Uncle Gus," but it was rumoured that she was really his girlfriend and that her husband did not know of the affair. On the evening of September 26, 1959, however, it was possibly chance that brought Janice and Pisano together. That night, she met up with a girlfriend at the Copacabana Night Club in New York, and Pisano turned up there as well.

The three then went along to Marino's, an Italian restaurant on Lexington Avenue, to meet others for dinner.

As it happened, Arlyne was at Marino's that evening too, hoping to hook up with a new love interest, Tony Mirra. Arlyne finally saw Mirra and another mobster pull up a chair at Pisano's table and sit down for a few minutes. She persisted in trying to get Mirra's attention and when she finally succeeded, he came over to her table quickly, threw some money down, and told her to leave, that he'd catch up with her later. Arlyne duly left.

After dinner, Pisano and Janice excused themselves, telling their companions they were going off to watch a televised boxing match. It was about 9:45 p.m. as Pisano drove his black 1959 Cadillac away from the restaurant.

Three-quarters of an hour later, shots rang out on 94th Street in the Queens section of New York City. Partly up on the curb, a black Cadillac still had its engine running when the first bystanders rushed to the scene. In the passenger seat was a blond woman leaning up against the door. She wore a low-cut cocktail dress, a fur stole, and lots of jewelry. She also had a bullet hole on the right side of her neck. Lying across her lap was the man who had been driving. He had a bullet hole in the left side of his neck and another in the back of his head. A fourth bullet pierced the windscreen.

Janice Drake and Little Augie Pisano were dead.

Hearing the shots, residents said they saw two men running away from the car, which had come to a stop. From the location of the bullets, police said the assassins must have been in the back seat of the car, suggesting the couple knew them.

Janice's thirteen-year-old son, Michael, was home alone when police arrived to say his mother had been murdered. Alan Drake, appearing with singer Tony Martin in a Washington club, rushed home. "I lost the greatest wife a man ever had," he sobbed after talking to the police. Janice was buried on September 29 and among the floral arrangements sent in her honor were ones from Tony Martin, Jerry Lewis, and Dean Martin.

With Pisano being who he was, there was no shortage of suspects. He even supplied a list himself. Tucked away in his pocket was a little red address book that turned out to be a Who's Who of the New York underworld. Rumors were that Pisano was at odds from the beginning with Don Vito Genovese, who had wanted all supporters of Frank Costello wiped out. Pisano had also been scheduled to appear shortly before a Senate Committee investigating racketeering.

No one was ever charged with the murders, but one person came forward more than 30 years later and said she knew who had done it. Interviewed for the 1992 book *Mob Girl*, by Tess Carpenter, Arlyne Weiss Brickman recounted how she was shocked to read about the murders the morning after she had just seen the victims at Marino's Restaurant. She also said she'd had an uneasy feeling about Mirra that night. A few days after the shootings, Mirra called Arlyne and sounded tense on the phone. He said he wanted her to meet him at a hotel, stressing she was to make sure she wasn't followed. When Arlyne arrived, Mirra told her he was hiding.

"What are you hiding from?" she asked

"Do you read the papers?"

"Yeah, I read the papers."

"Well, you know who killed Little Augie?"

"You?" She asked Mirra.

His silence told her everything. But why Janice, she asked.

"She was in the wrong place at the wrong time," Mirra replied.

The next day Arlyne was being questioned by a detective about her association with Mirra. The detective produced a list of names and as he went down the list, Arlyne acknowledged that she knew every one of them. The detective was not impressed.

"Who do you think you are?" he finally said to her. "Virginia Hill?"

Arlyne was in heaven.

Postscript: Following what she saw as a betrayal by the Mob in the 1970s, Arlyne Weiss Brickman spent the next twenty years as an informant, selling her information for money to law officials and testifying against mobsters.

Further reading

Andy Edmonds. *Bugsy's Baby*. New York: Carol Publishing Corporation, 1993.

E.R. Milner. *Lives and Times of Bonnie and Clyde*. Illinois: Southern Illinois University Press, 2003.

Steven Nickel and William J. Helmer. *Baby Face Nelson*. Tennessee: Cumberland House Publishing, Inc., 2002.

Ellen Poulsen. *Don't Call Us Molls*. New York: Clinton Cook Publishing Corp., 2002.

Phillip W. Steele and Marie Barrow Scoma. *The Family Story of Bonnie and Clyde*. Louisiana: Pelican Publishing Company, 2000.

John Toland. *The Dillinger Days*. Massachusetts: Da Capo Press, 1995.

Acknowledgments

I am always thankful to the writers who came before me, leaving me a trail of history to follow in news clippings, magazine articles, and books. I hope my own words linger as long.

Thanks to my editor/friend Georgina Montgomery, who always made my books more readable. Your skills have made me a much better writer.

I would like to acknowledge the resources of the websites of the *Chicago Tribune* and the *New York Times* and their historical archive divisions. For a writer, the ability to go back in time through their pages is invaluable.

I also want to thank Tessa Rose and the gang at Arcturus Publishing for helping to bring this book out into the world. I will be forever grateful.

Lastly, as always, many thanks to Jay and all the other cats in my life who have supported both me and my writing—you know who you are.

Index

INDEX

About the author

Susan McNicoll lives in Vancouver, British Columbia, Canada. Her lifelong love of words and history has been the main focus of her writing career, which began with five years as a reporter for the *Ottawa Journal* in the 1970s. She is the author of *The Opening Act: Canadian Theatre History 1945–1953, Jack the Ripper, British Columbia Murders, Ontario Murders* and *Toronto Murders*. Although her published work to date has been in the non-fiction realm, Susan is currently working on a series of fables based on the four seasons of healing. Visit her at www.susanmcnicoll.com